Handbook of Patrology

Patrick J. Hamell, M.A., D.D.
Vice President, St. Patrick's College, Maynooth

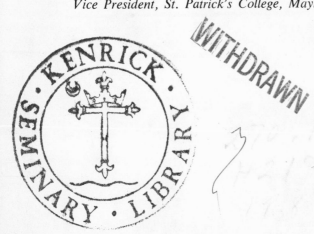

alba house alba house DIVISION OF THE SOCIETY OF ST. PAUL   STATEN ISLAND, N.Y. 10314

Printed and bound in the U.S.A. by the Pauline Fathers and Brothers of the Society of St. Paul at Staten Island, New York as a part of their communications apostolate.

CONTENTS

FOREWORD

The importance of Patrology in these days of growing interest in theology, especially the theology of a united Christendom, needs no proving. The story of the Fathers is the story of the Church as it came face to face with the world it was to evangelise and met the challenge not only of paganism but of heresy and schism, the story of the unfolding of Christian revelation. Their writings portray the life of the Church – the drama, the trials, the triumphs, the failures – and are themselves an expression of that life. For an understanding of what the Fathers wrote, the background of events, personalities, and mutual relations is even more necessary than for an appreciation of secular literature. This background is presented in a variety of excellent manuals, and it is greatly to be regretted that they are not used more widely. There is a real need for a concise, low-priced outline giving the essentials and pointing the way to further study.

This brief introduction is, in substance, notes compiled for the use of students attending lectures given by me in Maynooth College for some years. Their dependence on the work of others is obvious, and I gratefully acknowledge the debt I owe to the standard handbooks and other studies, especially to Bardenhewer-Shanan, Cayré-Howitt, Campbell, Tixeront-Raemers, Steidle, Altaner, Quasten. What is offered here is no more than an outline. It will have served its purpose if it introduces the Fathers and affords a glimpse of the treasures that reward deeper acquaintance with them.

My sincere thanks to my colleague, Dr. Michael Olden, who read the proofs and to James McEvoy, deacon, Maynooth College, who helped me greatly with the preparation of the text and read the proofs.

Patrick J. Hamell.

INTRODUCTION

Patrology is the science which deals with the life, writings, and doctrine of the orthodox writers of Christian antiquity. *Christian antiquity* means roughly the first eight centuries of the Church, including the period about the death of Charlemagne as well as the era of persecution, the ages of Constantine and Theodosius. It was really one, composed of two parts – Greek and Latin. As a result, the writers are venerated by the whole of Christendom.

Fathers. At first the title designated the heads of Churches, bishops, who were guardians both of disciplinary and doctrinal authority. Later, however, theological studies and treatises referred especially to the latter. The title came to designate defenders of the faith even though the authors were not bishops. Certain *qualifications* are necessary – four – and only some of the ecclesiastical writers are called Fathers of the Church: (a) *Orthodoxy of doctrine*, (2) *holiness of life*, (3) *ecclesiastical approval*, (4) *antiquity*. These marks refer to men who guarded the deposit of faith (1 *Tim.* 6,6). The title of Father, however, has been conferred on other writers who fulfilled only partially these conditions, e.g. Tertullian, Origen, Eusebius of Caesarea. The valuable services these men rendered to the Church explain their inclusion. We cannot define 'antiquity' precisely, but we shall confine our studies to the Patristic epoch and come to the death of St. John Damascene, Doctor of the Church, in the Greek section (c.A.D. 750), and St. Gregory the Great in the Latin (A.D. 540-604).

Doctors of the Church. This title is given to those authors who unite in themselves a profound knowledge of Christian doctrine, a rigid orthodoxy, and exemplary holiness of life, e.g. St. Basil, St. Gregory Naziazenus, St. Chrysostom – the Oecumenical Doctors (revered especially by the Byzantine Church) and St. Athanasius, St. Ambrose, St. Jerome, St. Augustine, St. Gregory the Great (eight 'great Doctors'). With the passing of Christian antiquity, we come to the Theologians and Doctors – from twelfth to sixteenth centuries.

Object of Patrology, Life, writings, doctrine of the Fathers of

9

the Church.

Life. The study of their life is important and useful, because it helps towards an understanding of their character and the circumstances under which their works were written.

Writings. These are part of the history of the authors. The first care is that they must be *authentic* – this is the province of the critics. An *analysis* of the writings must be made.

Doctrine. We should note: (1) the various points on which a Father insisted, points in which a step forward is made and which mark the writer as a pioneer; (2) his opinions on controverted questions of his day; (3) the points of his teaching requiring an explanation, favourable interpretation, or condemnation.

By means of this doctrinal synthesis Patrology is often linked up with the History of Dogma and Positive Theology. Dogma here does not mean all Christian doctrine but only revealed truths as proposed by the Church. The formulae containing these truths were the subject of controversies which provide matter for the History of Dogma. The Fathers played an important part in these controversies. Positive Theology concerns itself with showing, from Scripture and Tradition, that a truth is really revealed by God and defined by the Church, and supposes, therefore, acquaintance with the Fathers, and contributes to an understanding of their writings.

Doctrine comprises also the moral, ascetical and mystical teaching of the Fathers.

Method and Division. Only the great writers can be touched on in detail, the lesser authors being mentioned chiefly in relation to the more outstanding.

(a) *General division.* (1) *Language*-Latin, Greek, Syriac, Armenian and Coptic. The last three have numerous and sometimes important contributions, but Greek and Latin claim the majority and the most important authors.

(2) The study is based not on geographical or linguistic considerations but doctrine and history. (a) Intellectual kinship is important – those treating of same subjects are dealt with together, if possible; (b) chronology – the writers are not to be separated from their age.

(b) *Periods*: (1) The *origins* of Patristic literature – first, second and third centuries.

(2) *The Great Century.* The golden age of Patristic literature – 300 to 430.

(3) *The Last Centuries.* 430-850 or sixth-ninth centuries.

SUBDIVISIONS OF PATROLOGY

1. **Origins,** now the period of greatest interest. These authors living close to the founders of the Church are pre-eminent as *witnesses* to the traditional doctrines of the Trinity, Incarnation, the foundation, constitution and discipline of the Church. So the Apostolic Fathers (Part I) are most important. The last authors of Part I (2nd century) are also very important. The authors of the *third century* are far removed from the Apostolic Age but their attempts at systematisation of doctrine are highly important and make them the true forerunners of the great Doctors of the fourth century.

II. **The Second Period.** (A.D. 300-430) extends from St. Athanasius to the death of St. Augustine. In it appeared the most powerful minds in the history of the Church and there were fought out the great doctrinal controversies on the Trinity and Grace. Part I, 300-360 – the Trinitarian problem comes to the front. Part II, 360-430 – the great Doctors grapple with the difficulties raised by the Trinitarian problem and in such fashion that later centuries have but to record and uphold their teaching. Grace was also discussed.

III. **The Third Period.** (A.D. 430-850) – unfairly called the decadent centuries. *Section I* – the great Christological controversies – extends from the Council of Ephesus (431) to the second Council of Constantinople (553). These began with Apollinarism but it was during this century, during the rise and fall of semi-Pelagianism in the West, that the Councils and Doctors reached a definite solution. The authors of this age formed a link between the falling ancient world and the coming new world, and reach out to the men who were to enlighten the barbarians, to St. Gregory the Great in Italy, St. Gregory of Tours in Gaul, St. Isidore in Spain, the Venerable Bede in England. These provide the matter of Section II, with the last and more numerous Eastern writers whose work in the service of the Church (against Monothelitism) was considerable, though their style was inferior.

Importance of Patrology (a) The writings of the early Fathers are one of the *sources of doctrine*; they enshrine tradition. Criteria exist to determine when they speak as witnesses to

11

tradition which is, with the Bible, the source of Christian teaching.

(b) *Theological training* is incomplete without the elements of the History of Dogma and Positive Theology. All the great theologians studied the Fathers carefully, and reveal that in their works by extensive quotations. Theology is an explanation of the revealed data in Sacred Scripture, and is based on exegesis; and it was in the form of scriptural commentaries that it developed for many centuries, especially with the Fathers. So a study of the exegetical works of the Fathers is indispensable for the theologian and the exegete.

(c) *Christian unity.* All Christian bodies hold the Fathers in high esteem, and study of the Patristic writings should bring Christians to a better knowledge of Christ's teaching and promote unity.

(d) Patrology provides a synthesis which the division of ecclesiastical sciences into apparently independent and parallel branches may tend to conceal.

(e) Value to preachers is immense.

(f) In the works of the Fathers is an 'abundance of Christian feeling' (Bossuet). Each Father is a great Churchman – some men of deeds, some of doctrine, apologists and philosophers, mystics and saints, theologians and preachers. Some, like St. Augustine, combine all these talents in one powerful personality. Patrology presents a unique portrait gallery of holiness and learning.

THE TEXT OF THE FATHERS

The Patristic texts can be found in special editions containing either a single work or the complete works of each author. Those editions began in the sixteenth century and improved in the seventeenth and eighteenth centuries. The Benedictines of St. Maur des Fosses are worthy of special mention for their distinguished scholarship.

Single Collections of several writers began with **Marguerin de la Bigne** (d. 1589). In his *Bibliotheca Sanctorum Patrum* he collected the works of more than 200 early or medieval writers. This collection gradually increased and in Cologne in 1616 it had become the *Magna Bibliotheca Veterum Patrum* in 14 vols. – later re-edited at Lyons in 27 volumes (1677) *Maxima Bibliotheca V.P. et antiq. scriptorum ecclesiasticorum.*

The Oratorian, **A. Galland** (d. 1779), published his *Bibliotheca Veterum Patrum* in Venice in 1765-81, and 1788 (14 vols.). In the 19th century **M. J. Routh** (*Reliquiae Sacrae*, 1814, Oxford), Cardinals *A. Mai, S.J.* and *J. Pitra, O.S.B.*, are outstanding.

Migne

The **Abbé Migne** (d. 1875) compiled the greatest and most important collection of all – *Patrologiae Cursus Completus* (PG, PL) – which is immense and needs substantial re-editing. His purpose was not to publish the unpublished or to revise, but to collect the majority of the known works. *Latin Patrology* contains 217 vols. and 4 vols. of Indexes (to Pope Innocent III, d. 1216) – Greek (with Latin translation) goes as far as the Council of Florence (1439) and contains 161 vols. No. 162 was never printed, as a fire destroyed all the founts while it was being printed. The Latin series was published from 1844-1855 and Greek from 1857-1866. A general index was made later (Paris, 1912).

Patrologia Latina: Supplementum (PLS).
For the first 96 vols. of Migne (Patres Latini) Father A. Hamman is preparing a *Patrologia Latina*: Supplementum in 4 vols. Vol I has already been published by Editions Brepols, Turn-

hout (Belgium). The publishers are contemplating a supplement to the Greek Fathers also. (See P. Glorieux, 'Pour Revaloriser Migne – Tables rectificatives', *Mélanges de Science Religieuse* 9 (1952) Cahier Supplémentaire.)

Father A. Hamman, who sees the Migne collection of texts, excursus etc. as essential because continuing the humanist tradition of the Renaissance scholars and the Benedictine monks, conceived the project of correcting erroneous attributions of ownership, of re-grouping works separated without justification and furnishing the latest results of scholarly criticism for disputed writings, and thus retaining Migne and making the collection as useful as possible. Hundreds of texts forgotten by the original editors or discovered later and now scattered in individual works and difficult of access, will be added. The first 96 vols. of Migne will be revised in this way, and the reader will have a volume (PLS) which he can use to correct Migne as he reads. The project is to cover 1-96 (Tertullian-Bede). PLS 1 has been completed and is published in four fascicules, Paris, 1958-9 and covers PL 1-21 PLS 2 will cover PL 22-48; PLS 3 will cover PL 49-65; PLS 4 will cover PL 66-96.

Patrologia Graeca – reissue of Migne, MPG at present is made up of: (1) the original edition; (2) reprints of a certain number of volumes after the fire of 1868, many misprints etc.; (3) photomechanical reproductions made since 1904 of volumes out of print, of poor quality. Dom Olivier Rousseau reported to the Patristic Conference, 1959, his project of a photomechanical reproduction, but of much better standard, of volumes no longer available.

Collections and Translations

(a) Collections which supplement Migne:
Patrologia Syriaca, by R. Griffin. Paris, 1894 ff., 3 vols.
Patrologia Orientalis, by R. Griffin and F. Nau. Paris, 1903 ff., 28 vols.
Corpus scriptorum christianorum Orientalium, by J. Chabot, 1903 I. Guidi, H. Hyvernat, B. Carra de Vaux, Forget. Paris, 1903 ff. Louvain-Washington, 228 vols.
(b) Collections which supplement and revise Migne:
Corpus scriptorum ecclesiasticorum latinorum, edited by the Academy of Vienna, 1866 ff., 78 vols, Latin text only.

14

Monumenta Germaniae historica, Auctores antiquissimi,
Berlin, 1877 ff., 13 vols. (later Latin writers up to the Middle
Ages).

Die Griechischen christlichen Schriftsteller (Greek Christian
writers of the first three centuries), Berlin, 1897 ff.

Bibliotheca Teubneriana, Leipzig.

Loeb Classical Library, edd. Page, Capps, Rouse. London-
New York 1912.

Sources chrétiennes, edd. H. de Lubac, J. Danielou. Paris,
1941 ff.

Corpus Christianorum. Series latina, Turnhout: Brepols.
1954 ff., c. 30 vols.

Corpus Christianorum under the Benedictines of Steenbrugge
promises to be the most comprehensive collection since Migne.
It was announced in *Sacris Erudiri I* (1948), pp. 405-414. The
first volume appeared in 1953 from Ed. Brepols. The collection
is to have 175 vols. covering Latin writing of the first eight
centuries, including mat⁺er in the first 96 vols. of Migne PL.
See 'A Proposed New Edition of the Christian Texts' by
Patrick J. Hamell, *Irish Ecc. Record,* November 1948, pp.
990-3, from which the following is quoted. 'The editors have a
twofold proposal to make: 'the publication of a *Manuductio
ad litteraturam patristicam,* which will indicate the best editions
extant of all the written documents of Christian antiquity;
2. the issue, with the consent of the publishers and their
eventual compensation, of a new collection of all early Christian texts, according to the best editions, more or less on the
lines laid down by Dom Pitra and the Abbé Migne, now a
hundred years ago'.

The 'new Migne' will contain only the text and its variants,
with a very brief Latin Introduction giving essential data
concerning authenticity, date, manuscript, tradition etc. and
a select bibliography. The indices appended will be the best
ancient indices in adapted form or new indices. The pagination
of the text employed will be given and, where necessary, the
pagination of another widely circulated edition, e.g. the Vienna
edition. Every early Christian text will be reproduced in the
Corpus Christianorum, and anti-Christian and pagan authors
will find a place also and the most important of the pagan
historians dealing with Christianity, e.g. Procopius and
Ammianus Marcellinus.

The editors contemplate a *series graeca* (CCG) and a *series
latina* (CCL), and hope that 'ten years will be sufficient for the

publication of the one hundred and twenty octavo volumes contemplated for the Latin series'. (The figure 120 has been revised to 180).

With *Corpus Christianorum* should be linked:
1. A revised edition of the *Clavis patrum latinorum*, 1951, announced for 1961. It is CC's 'basic instrument de travail' (Burghardt).
2. *Excerpta in usum, scholarum seorsum edita*, extracts from CCL volumes, for seminar use.
3. *Instrumenta patristica* – providing the tools of research useful in editing of texts.
4. *Continuatio mediaevalis* – it is to correct and complete PL 97-217.

Scriptores Latini Hiberniae (SLH), published by the Institute for Advanced Studies, Dublin, 1955 ff. (Bieler, Binchy, Gwynn) – purpose is to provide reliable texts and translations of the sources for the study of the Latin culture of medieval Ireland. Vol. I (1955) is: *The Writings of Bishop Patrick*, 1075-1084, by Aubrey Gwynn. SLH 2 is *Sancti Columbani Opera* (Walker, 1957). SLH 3 is Adamnan's 'De cunctis locis' (Denis Meehan, 1958). SLH 4 is *Itinerarium fratris Symonis*. *The Irish Penitentials* (Bieler-Binchy) and several other titles to follow. See *Theological Studies*, March, 1955, 1960.

Reallexikon für Antike ünd Christentum (RAC) – purpose is to describe how early Christianity came to terms with the heritage of the ancient world. It is in the form of a dictionary. In articles appearing under key words it gives a picture of the life of the first six centuries. 4 vols. had appeared in 1960. See *Theological Studies*, March 1955, 1960.

Verba Seniorum is a collection of patristic and medieval texts designed to present first-hand knowledge of religious thought of the era by presenting the outstanding personalities. Turin. See *Theological Studies*, March 1956.

Bibliographia Patristica is a project undertaken by scholars to provide a continuous bibliography of patristic literature, collecting material from all publications, Vol. 1 appeared in 1956. See *Theological Studies*, March 1960.

For information on current projects see *Theological Studies* (Woodstock, Md.) Vol. 17 and Vol. 21, March 1956, 1960, where Father W. Burghardt, S.J. writes on reports made to the Second and Third International Conference on Patristic Studies, Oxford (1955, 1959).

16

(c) Smaller Collections:

S.S. Patrum opuscula selecta, by H. Hurter, Innsbruck, Series I, 1868-1885, 48 vols.; Series 2, 1884-1892, 6 vols.

Textes et Documents pour l'étude historique au christianisme, by H. Hemmer and P. Lejay, (text, transl.) Paris, 1904.

Sammlung ausgewählter k.u.d. Quellenschriften, by G. Krüger, Tübingen, 1891-1896 and 1901 ff.

Kleine Texte, ed. H. Leitzmann, Bonn, 1902 ff.

Florilegium Patristicum, ed. G. Rauschen. Bonn, 1904 ff.

Cambridge Patristic Texts, ed. A. Mason. Cambridge, 1899 ff.

Bibliotheca sanctorum Patrum, ed. J. Vizzini. Roma, 1902 ff.

Corona Patrum Salesiana, Turin, 1936 ff.

Anthologia patristica Graeca, Turin, 1931.

Textus et Documenta, Universitas Gregoriana, Roma, 1932 ff.

Enchiridion Patristicum, ed. M. J. Rouet de Journel, 21st Edition, Freiburg, 1960. (Cf. *Enchiridion Asceticum and Enchiridion Symbolorum* and *Thesaurus doctrinae catholicae* (Cavallera)).

Documents of the Christian Church, ed. H. Bettenson. London, 1947.

Textos del Christianismo primitivo y Santos Padres (Biblioteca Autores Cristianos, Madrid (c. 1950).

English Translations

Library of the Fathers (Pusey-Keble-Newman). Oxford, 1838-1888, 45 vols.

The Ante-Nicene Christian Library (Roberts-Donaldson-Menzies). Edinburgh, 1866-1897, 25 vols.

A Select Library of Nicene and Post-Nicene Fathers of the Christian Church (Schaff-Wace). New York, 1886-1900, 28 vols.

Translations of Christian Literature (Sparrow-Simpson and Lowther Clarke) (SPCK). 1917 ff., London.

Fathers of the Church (selected writings of the Latin Fathers). F. A. Wright, London, 1928.

Ancient Christian Writers (Quasten-Plumpe). Westminster, Md., 1946 ff.

The Fathers of the Church (Schopp). New York, 1947 ff.

The Early Christian Fathers (Selection). H. Bettenson, London, 1956.

17

STUDIES OF THE FATHERS

Patrology is an ancient science, ecclesiastical literature with emphasis on the matter rather than the literary form. The first manual of it goes back to St. Jerome, *De Viris Illustribus* (393) (akin to the work Suetonius had done 200 years before for secular literature). St. Jerome relied somewhat on Eusebius's *Church History* but St. Jerome's work forms the basis of our authority and for centuries remained the standard work. After him we have Gennadius of Marseilles, St. Isidore of Seville, St. Ildephonsus, Photius, etc.

FIRST PERIOD
(Saec. I-III)

I. Primitive Ecclesiastical Literature

The Apostles' Creed (Symbolum Apostolicum)
The Didache or Teaching of the Twelve Apostles

Apostolic Fathers

Works in Greek
St. Clement of Rome (?-102?). *Epistola ad Corinthios* (c. 96).
Opera adscripta (1) *Ep. 2 ad Corinthios* (2) *Epistolae I-II Ad Virgines*.
   St. Ignatius of Antioch (?-107). Seven epistles.
   St. Polycarp of Smyrna (70?-156). Epistle to the Philippians, etc.
   Papias of Hierapolis (c. 130). 'Explanation of the Oracles of Our Lord'.
   The so-called Epistle of Barnabas (end of first century, at Alexandria?).
   The Shepherd of Hermas   (Hermas lived in the second century.)

II. Apologetic Literature of the Second Century

Quadratus. (c. 124). Asia Minor.
Aristides of Athens. (c. 125)
Aristo of Pella. (c. 140).
St. Justin Martyr. (c. 165).
Tatian the Assyrian. (post 172?).
Miltiades. (c. 192).
Apollinaris of Hierapolis. (c. 172).

Melito of Sardis. (c. 190).
Athenagoras of Athens. (c. 177).
Theophilus of Antioch. (post 181). Syria.
The Letter to Diognetus (2nd or 3rd century).
Hermias. (c. 200).
Minucius Felix. (2nd or 3rd century).

III. The Heretical Literature of the Second Century and the New Testament Apocrypha

Gnostic Literature; Judaistic Literature; Montanist Literature;

New Testament Apocrypha: Apocryphal Gospels, Acts of the Apostles, Letters of the Apostles, Apocalypses.

IV. Anti-Heretical Literature of the Second Century

Anti-Gnostics. Lost works
St. Irenaeus of Lyons. (c. 140-c. 202). *Anti-Montanists.*
Writings of Ecclesiastical Authorities and Synods.

V. Ecclesiastical Literature During the Genesis of Christian Theology

Eastern Writers
A. **Alexandrines.** Clement of Alexandria (c. 125). Origen (c. 185-254-55). Dionysius of Alexandria (d.c. 264). The later authorities of the catechetical school of Alexandria. The so-called Apostolic Church-Ordinance (3rd century-end).
B. **Syro-Palestinians.** Julius Africanus (d. post 240). Paul of Samosata (c. 260). Malchion of Antioch (c. 268). Lucian of Samosata (m. 312). Pamphilus of Caesarea (d. 309) and the *Dialogus de recta in Deum fide* (c. 310). The *Didascalia Apostolorum* (3rd century).
C. **Writers of Asia Minor.** St. Gregory Thaumaturgus (c. 213-c. 270). St. Methodius of Olympus (m. 311).

Western Writers
A. **African.** Tertullian (c. 160-c. 220). St. Cyprian (c. 200?-258). Arnobius (c. 280-c. 310). Lactanius (d. post 317).
B. **Roman.** Hippolytus (c. 160-235). Church Orders. Novatian (d. post 251). Papal Letters.
C. **Others**: Commodian (c. 250). Victorinus of Pettau (d. 304) and Recticius of Autun (c. 313). Acts of the Martyrs.

I. PRIMITIVE ECCLESIASTICAL LITERATURE

The writings of this period are meagre. It was not the mission of the Christian teachers to write. Oral teaching was the important thing and it was due to special circumstances that the New Testament literature came into being. After it, oral teaching still remained the normal method of imparting and spreading the Christian truth. The non-canonical writings of the first two Christian generations are called Apostolic and their authors were known as *Apostolic Fathers*. These men knew the Apostles or their immediate successors and their authority is great, especially now when so much interest is centred on the early years of Christianity. They are the first witnesses to the early faith and reliable because the works are not the fruit of personal speculation, but a reflection of the circumstances in which they were written. They are an immediate echo of the Apostles' teaching. This is shown by the abundance of Scripture quotations – Old and New Testament alike quoted. *Doctrine* – little method in it, a few fundamental ideas, *Trinity and Incarnation* – God one and three; Jesus Christ true God and true man; the Church a Christian society organised hierarchically with full powers in the name of God. Moral teaching is strongly tinged with asceticism.

THE APOSTLES' CREED

The Apostles' Creed is a profession of faith used, with certain variations for the instruction of catechumens, from the beginning of the sixth century in France and Spain, and a little later in Ireland and Germany. It is not inspired, and has never been considered as canonical, but is very important. It is an official document of belief. 'Although this liturgical and catechetical monument is not, in its present form, a synodal and theological document, it is the infallible expression of the daily teaching of the Church' (A. Vacant). Numerous studies have been made of the Creed – Rufinus, Nicetas of Remesiana, in the West, and St. Cyril of Jerusalem, in the East, later St. Augustine and St. Peter Chrysologus. Important modern names – Holl, Harnack, Lake, and others mentioned below.

21

See *Early Christian Creeds* by J. N. D. Kelly.

The text which is admitted at present does not date from the beginning of the Church. There is a difference between it and the text given in the commentary of Rufinus of Aquileia written about 404 and the first to be known in the West. According to tradition the ancient text of the Creed goes back to the Apostles not only in contents but verbally. The Greek version is the oldest we have; our authority is to be found in a letter of Marcellus, bishop of Ancyra, to Pope Julius I, written in 337 or 338. The text of Rufinus is called the *Roman text*, as opposed to the *Gallican text*. The latter is the one actually in use and it is found almost entire in the work of St. Caesarius of Arles (d. 543). The variants in use were finally reduced to a single formula which at a later and unknown date (probably 5th or 6th century) found its way into the Roman liturgy. Caspari showed that the ancient baptismal creed of the Roman Church is the common basis and root of all the primitive baptismal creeds of the West, and Kattenbusch holds that the Roman creed was also the archetype of all Eastern creeds. It is agreed that the contents of the old Creed are apostolic but it is not possible to prove the phraseology goes back to the Apostles – nor is it possible to prove it does not. It is certain that from the earliest days of the Church the need of some kind of profession of faith before the reception of baptism was felt. The convert had to give expression of his faith in the fundamental doctrines and it must be admitted, with Caspari, that the ancient Roman Creed 'with its primitive severity, its extreme simplicity and brevity, its highly lapidary style, impresses us as a document that has come down, word for word, from the most remote Christian antiquity.'

Father J. de Ghellinck, S.J. (*Patristique et moyen âge I*. Les Recherches sur les origines du Symbole des Apôtres. 1946) emphasises that the Creed's important place in early times, especially in Baptism, shows the dogmatic nature of Christianity. Not love and religious brotherhood merely were preached. Catholic and non-Catholic scholars agree that the content of the Creed goes back to apostolic times and the Creed was used as a baptismal formula from the beginning. Without it one could not become a Christian. (1) In 1483 Eastern spokesmen at Ferrara told the West that they had no Apostles' Creed. The humanist L. Valla, d. 1457, criticised a friar in Naples for teaching that the Apostles taught the articles – the accepted explanation since the time of Rufinus. Erasmus (1517) held the

22

date 325 as the earliest. In 1647 Archbishop Ussher showed that the formula of the Creed in use in his day differed from the formula in Rome in the fourth century, the articles on descent into hell and the communion of saints not being found in the Roman formula, G. Voss confirmed this. (2) A new phase opened in 1842 with Hahn and Caspari (1860-90), Kattenbusch, Harnack, Burn, Loofs. By 1914 it was agreed that the ancient Roman form discovered by Ussher could be traced to about 100. It had been used as a baptism formula in Rome for 300 years after that and gave place to the Nicaea-Constantinople Creed. From Rome in the second century and third it went to Gaul, with the two clauses – then back to Rome and was re-adopted in the ninth century. In the East there was less uniformity, at least before the last quarter of the third century. The place of origin of the Ancient Roman Formula was Rome or Asia Minor, in the circle of St. John the Evangelist. (3) The last phase began in 1918 with Peitz, Nussbaumer and Haussleiter. Previous investigations had assumed the ancient Roman formula (ARF) to have been a single unit from the beginning. The findings of these three at the same time seem to prove that before the appearance of ARF (also called R) there had existed two parallel formulae – one shorter and strictly Trinitarian in content, the other longer, historical and principally Christological in content. Peitz used *Liber Diurnus* and Nussbaumer used Justin and Irenaeus, Haussleiter used *Liber Diurnus* and Apostolic Fathers and the New Testament, and all three concluded that ARF was a fusion of two pre-existent formulae. The theory was criticised but accepted in regard to the main thesis. In 1910-1940 the outstanding name is Lietzmann, and Catholic names appear prominently. Dom Connolly, Dom Capell, J. Lebreton specialised in this field. From 1842-1942 de Ghellinck reckons 400 publications on the Creed. Lebreton 'hazarded the guess that the pontificate of Victor (189-197) may well have witnessed the final redaction of 'R'' (ARF) (Kelly, o.c., p. 130), and that 'the claims of a slightly earlier date than the reign of Pope Victor deserve to be considered... The underlying formula on which it (R) was based was in all probability a simple three-clause interrogation modelled on... the Matthaean baptismal command; thus it joins hands with the faith and practice of the first century Church. The Christology which was later combined with it was a sample of that semi-stereotyped proclamation of the good news about Christ which second-century Christians had in-

23

herited practically unaltered from the Apostles'. (Kelly,o.c., p. 130).

THE DIDACHE

The Didache. The Teaching of the Twelve Apostles, (Didache ton dodeka apostolon; Didache ton Kuriou dia ton dodeka apostolon tois Ethnesi; *Doctrina Domini Gentibus per Duodecim Apostolos*).

History. The first is an abridgement of the second and original title – an abstract of Christ's teaching as presented to the Gentiles by the Apostles. The complete text of this book of religious instruction was discovered in 1873 by Bryennios, Greek Orthodox Metropolitan of Nicomedia, in the Jerusalem Codex (A.D. 1052 or 1056) and was published in 1883. (Barnabas and St. Clement of Rome were discovered also.) It was known by name, and in part (by quotation), from Clement of Alexandria, Origen, and St. Athanasius. It is undoubtedly one of the oldest documents, if not the oldest, of Christian antiquity. In the early Church, especially in Egypt and Syria and Palestine, the *Didache* was very highly esteemed. Clement of Alexandria cites it as 'Scripture'. Eusebius places it amongst the spurious works. St. Athanasius recommends it as very useful to catechumens. The so-called Apostolic Church Ordinance (3rd century, in Egypt) paraphrases the description of the Way of Life – there is also borrowing from the Didache in the Apostolic Constitutions (4th century, Syria). Amongst the Latins the work is the first met with in the pseudo-Cyprianic homily *Adversus aleatores*. There is extant a Latin version of Chaps. 1-6 (published by J. Schlecht).

The **Author** is unknown. He may have borrowed from the description of the Two Ways in the Epistle of Barnabas – or vice versa – possibly, but unlikely, both borrowed from an older source. There is no ground for a theory of borrowing from a Jewish work – no evidence for such a work – and the *Didache* is specifically Christian in character. *Time and Place of Composition*. It was probably composed in the last decades of the first century or before 120, in Syria or Palestine, or Egypt. From the primitive condition of the liturgy and of the hierarchy there is an argument for placing it as near as possible to the Apostolic times. The conditions regarding rites of Baptism, Eucharist, ministers of the divine mysteries *(episcopoi kai*

24

diakonoi) and ministers of the divine word *(apostoloi kai prophetai)* are no longer met with in the second century.

Contents. A. (chapters 1-10) contains ecclesiastical ritual of the time, 1-6 Instruction in Christian Ethics containing description of the Two Ways – of Life (1-4) and Death (5). This is given to guide those who seek Baptism. Treatment of Baptism, fasting and prayer and of the Blessed Eucharist.

B. (chapters 10-16) deals with the mutual relations of the Christian communities – scrutiny of wandering Christian teachers, reception of travelling brethren, support of prophets and teachers in the community, religious life of each community (e.g. divine service on Sunday) and the superiors of the communities. Chapter 16 exhorts watching in preparation for the last day which is at hand. (See Dr. W. J. Philbin's 'The Didache and its Critics', *Irish Ecc. Record*, January 1941).

THE SO-CALLED EPISTLE OF BARNABAS

Contents. Current under the name of St. Paul's companion it gives neither the name of author or recipients nor their dwelling-place. It is divided into two main parts: (1) Chaps. 2-17, and (2) Chaps. 18-20. It was evidently composed for those Christians who were in danger of being seduced by Judaisers, and seeks to give a purely spiritual interpretation of the Old Testament. (1) The author asserts that the Old Testament was never valid and that Judaism was a work of human folly and the devil. God asked not for sacrifice but a contrite heart, avoidance of sin, etc. (2) A setting forth of the Two Ways – Light and Darkness – as in the *Didache.*

Author. Christian antiquity (Clement of Alexandria, Origen, Eusebius, St. Jerome) ascribed it to St. Barnabas (though it did not regard it as inspired). Modern opinion is against this. It would be out of character for St. Barnabas to write in this manner about the Old Testament. The teaching of the Old Testament is opposed to the Apostolic teaching – St. Paul's especially. Besides, the date of composition excludes St. Barnabas, who certainly did not survive the destruction of Jerusalem (70), a date looked on by the author as already past (c. 16). St. Barnabas was no longer alive in the time of Nerva (96-98) when the letter is generally agreed to have been written. The reign of Hadrian (117-138) is a possibility, too. Steidle places it between 100 and 120. M. d'Herbigny (because of c. 5) places it during Vespasian's reign, shortly after the destruction of the Temple. The place of composition is usually understood to be Alexandria – allegorical interpretation of Scripture was much in vogue there.

ST. CLEMENT OF ROME

St. Clement of Rome. *Life.* According to St. Irenaeus (*Adv. Haer.* III, 3) St. Clement was fourth bishop of Rome (St. Peter, St. Linus, St. Anacletus). Eusebius, relying on St. Irenaeus and Hegisippus, places Linus 68-80; Anacletus 80-92, and St. Clement 92-101. It is likely that he was of Jewish parentage, and not belonging to the imperial family of the Flavians. It cannot be proved that he was St. Paul's colleague (*Philippians*, 4.3) but he seems to have been a disciple of the Apostles in Rome. He was a man of authority practised in government, a man of moderation and generosity. He was, according to tradition, a martyr.

Letter to the Corinthians. It is the only authentic writing of St. Clement. It has reached us in the Greek original and in a Latin and a Syriac version. In Corinth trouble had arisen and some members had revolted and driven out the rulers of the Church, and there was a danger of this Church founded by St. Paul being permanently divided and destroyed. Clement, as bishop of Rome, wrote to re-establish peace and order. First he describes the former flourishing state of the Church and refers to the present deplorable conditions. There are sixty-five chapters in all. Chapters 1-4 Exordium; 4-62 Body; 62-65 Conclusion. Pt. I (cc. 4-36), instruction of a general character, warns the Corinthians against envy and jealousy, recommends humility and obedience and appeals to the types and examples of these virtues in the Old Testament. Pt. II (cc. 36-61) deals more directly with the situation at Corinth. It treats of the ecclesiastical hierarchy and shows the necessity of subjection to the legitimate ecclesiastical authorities. Conclusion (62-65) summarises what he has already said.

The letter does not contain St. Clement's name; it is written in the name of the Christian community at Rome, but there is abundant evidence that Clement wrote it as head of the Roman church. St. Dionysius, bishop of Corinth about 170, wrote to Pope Soter: 'Today we have celebrated the Lord's holy day, in which we have read you letter. From it, whenever we read it, we shall always be able to draw advice, as also from the former letter which was written to us by Clement'. We have the testimony of Hegesippus and St. Irenaeus; also, St. Polycarp, without quoting the letter, imitated it in his letter to the Philippians. The letter of Clement was composed probably towards the end of Domitian's reign (81-96) or the beginning of Nerva's (96-98), probably during the aftermath of Domitian's persecution which ended in 95 or 96.

Importance. This letter is very important in Christian doctrine as a witness to the *primacy of the Roman Church*. It seems unlikely (chaps. 1 and 47) that Rome was asked to intervene, and unasked intervention with the conviction that the restoration of order was a duty incumbent on Rome is explicit testimony to the authority of Rome. The Church of Rome offers no excuses, but supposes it has even been neglecting a duty in not writing before now; it threatens, and indicates that it wishes to be obeyed. If Rome was asked, this is very remarkable seeing that St. John was still living. Lastly, the welcome given to the letter shows the Corinthians did not think Rome had overstepped its powers.

Ecclesiastical Hierarchy. The information on this is chiefly in chaps. 42-44 – its institution, chap. 42. *Episcopi and presbyteri* with deacons to aid them, established for each community by the Apostles. Succession was provided for – the Christian ministry was authoritatively transmitted to new *episcopi* whom the community has not the right to remove.

The so-called Second Letter to the Corinthians is a homily ascribed to Clement (c. 140-150) preached probably at Corinth. Some maintain it is a letter of Pope Soter to Corinth (166-174). (Cf. Eusebius, Hist. 4, 23, 11.) It is very general in character – the Christian must lead a life worthy of his calling, etc. Eusebius mentions it as purporting to be the second letter of Clement, but suspected its origin. It was published in 1875.

The Two Letters to Virgins have been ascribed to Clement also. They have reached us in Syriac, but are probably from a Greek original and were probably written in Syria or Palestine in the third century. They are addressed to unmarried persons, of both sexes. Lengthy fragments of a Greek text of both letters were discovered in 1884 in the 'Pandects' (summaries) of the Palestinian monk, Antiochus (c. 620-).

ST. IGNATIUS OF ANTIOCH

St. Ignatius of Antioch (?-107), called Theophoros (God-bearer), the third bishop of Antioch (after St. Peter and Evodius), was brought to Rome under Trajan (98-117) and exposed to wild beasts. On the way to Rome he wrote seven Letters to the Christians of Ephesus, Magnesia, Tralles, Rome, Philadelphia, Smyrna, and to Polycarp, bishop of Smyrna. There have been numerous collections of these letters – the biggest containing seven genuine and six spurious letters (the *Long Recension*). This seems to be the work of an Apollinarist forger in the fourth of fifth century. There is a *Mixed Recension* – seven genuine and six spurious (still extant in a Greek original and a Latin version). The genuine collection is in this recension. There is besides a small collection, and an Armenian version.

The text of these letters offers some difficulty in describing the versions. See Cayré-Howitt, Quasten, who differ in terminology. The facts are as follows. There are seven genuine letters and their authenticity is guaranteed by Polycarp and Eusebius (who gives the contents of the letters and the order given above). In the fourth century an Apollinarist (or Arian?) forger inserted interpolations into the genuine letters and added six quite spurious letters, making the collection thirteen letters, and this became known as the *long recension* and was the version that became known first. It was printed in Latin in 1489 and in Greek in 1557. This was the only work attributed to Ignatius and grave doubts were held about its authenticity.

In 1646 Archbishop Ussher (Armagh) discovered and published the primitive text of six of Ignatius's Letters and in 1689 Dom Ruinart discovered and published the primitive text of the *Letter to the Romans* (the missing seventh). The discoveries raised a storm of controversy in Catholic and Protestant circles (doctrines of hierarchy, Rome, Eucharist). This (the seven genuine plus the six) was known as the *mixed recension*. The *short recension* properly is the original seven (without interpolations and without the six spurious letters) and it exists in Greek only. Cureton published three of the letters in 1845 (original, primitive). Lightfoot in 1885 definitely established the authenticity of the Ignatian epistles in the *mixed recension*.

Contents. On his journey Ignatius made a lengthy stay at Smyrna and met representatives from several communities of

Asia Minor and he gave the representatives of Ephesus, Magnesia and Tralles letters for these communities telling them to beware of heretics and to submit to ecclesiastical authority. He sent from Smyrna a letter to Rome telling them not to try and save him. 'I fear that your love will cause me a damage' (1.2). 'For I shall not have such another occasion to enter into the possession of God' (2.1). 'I am the wheat of God, and I must be ground by the teeth of wild beasts that I may become the pure bread of God' (4.1). He calls Rome the community that 'presides over the society of love', i.e. the whole Church. From Troas he wrote to Philadelphia and Smyrna and to Polycarp. 'I cried out with a loud voice, with the voice of God: hold fast to the bishop, to the presbytery, to the deacons' (Phil. 7.1). 'Wherever the bishop is, there let the people be, as wherever Jesus Christ is, there is the Catholic Church' (Smyrn. 8.2.). ('Catholic Church' is met here for the first time in sense of the whole body of the faithful.) From Troas he went to martyrdom. 'His literary remains are the outpouring of a pastoral heart, aflame with a consuming love for Jesus Christ and His Church. The style is original and extremely vivacious – while the strong emotions of the writer frequently interfere with the ordinary forms of expression. Very frequently he reminds us of certain epistles of the Apostle of the Gentiles'. (Bardenhewer).

Authenticity of the epistles was keenly contested chiefly because the monarchical episcopate envisaged in them was conceived by the liberal Protestants not to have been then in existence. The discovery of the different recensions caused the question to pass through different phases. Today even the principal non-Catholic scholars, Zahn, Lightfoot, Harnack, maintain the authenticity of the Letters. Irenaeus refers to a passage in the *Letter to the Romans* (4.1.). Lucian of Samosata, *De Morte Peregrini* (A.D. 167) seems to have used the letters. St. Polycarp (c. 156) writes to the Philippians: 'The letters of Ignatius that he sent us – we have sent to you, according to your wish...' To get rid of St. Ignatius's letters some have denied the authenticity of St. Polycarp's letter. Opponents argued that Ignatius's portrait has been disfigured by the addition of impossible features; that heresy was not important then; that the ecclesiastical constitution described there did not exist then. The position of a bishop is given with great precision, as distinct from the presbyters, the episcopate as monarchical and not collegiate. Irenaeus, however, was able to compile a catalogue of the bishops of Rome going back to the Apostles and so it is impossible to hold that the episcopate begins only in the second century. The Letters were not forged in the interest of the episcopate – the episcopate is set forth as well established and accepted. In regard to heresy, there was heresy (Cerinthus's heresy) in St. John's lifetime. The supposed lack of naturalness in St. Ignatius's person is a mystery if such a figure had been created by a forger. The *importance* of the Letters is evident. The position of the *bishop* has already been noted. He is one and in supreme authority. He is first, the priests second, deacons third. The bishop has duties as well as rights. *Rome's privileges* are stressed. *Christ* is the centre of all St. Ignatius's teaching.

Heresy of Judaizers and Docetists is mentioned and the heresy of the latter brings into prominence the *Incarnation of the Word* – and the reality of the Eucharistic Body.

The *spiritual life* is imbued throughout by the thought of the presence of Christ. Christians are *God-bearers, Christ-bearers*. Lastly there is expressed contempt of self with a profound knowledge of Christ.

ST. POLYCARP OF SMYRNA

St. Polycarp of Smyrna (70?-156). We learn from St. Irenaeus that he had listened as a boy to St. Polycarp and had 'heard him tell of his relations with John (the Apostle) and with others who had seen the Lord, and how he quoted from their language and how much he had learned from them concerning the Lord and his miracles and his teaching' (in Euseb., *Hist. Ecc.* v. 20.6). Polycarp visited Rome in 154 or early in 155, hoping to bring about agreement with Pope Anicetus concerning the celebration of Easter – without success. He is said to have converted some followers of Marcion and Valentinus to the true faith. Polycarp died a martyr's death at Smyrna at eighty-six, A.D. 155 or 156 (on 23 February).

The **Epistle to the Philippians** is St. Polycarp's answer to the letter which the Philippians had addressed to him after the visit of St. Ignatius. St. Irenaeus tells us of 'a very excellent letter of Polycarp to the Philippians...' We have fragments of the original Greek and the entire text of an old Latin translation. It encourages this community to constancy (at Philippi, in Macedonia) and stresses certain duties of married people, widows, deacons, youths, virgins, clergy. It is full of imitations of St. Clement's letter to Corinth and as late as end of fourth century it was read in some places in Asia Minor at divine service (St. Jerome, *De Vir. Illus*, c. 17). Its literary value is not great, nor its theological value. Its chief importance is its guarantee of the authenticity of St. Ignatius's Letters. A. Lelong says that there is practically no other early writing which has better evidence of being authentic.

Marytrium S. Polycarpi. These 'Acts' relate his martyrdom with great detail, and are a letter written the year after his death by **Marcion** relating that St. Polycarp was burned alive and had a dagger thrust through his body. The Christians gathered his ashes and celebrated his memory on his anniversary. The 'Acts' are genuine beyond doubt and one of the oldest accounts of martyrdom.

PAPIAS OF HIERAPOLIS

Papias of Hierapolis (Phrygia), 'a hearer' of St. John, and friend of Polycarp (Irenaeus, *Adv. Haer.*, v. 33,4) wrote about 130:

'Explanations of the sayings of the Lord' (logion kuriakon exegeseis) in five books. In them he treats of the origin of the Gospels of St. Mathew and St. Mark, and of the witnesses on whom he depends. Amongst those he names John, and the question arose 'de utroque Johanne' (John the Apostle, and John the Presbyter). St. Irenaeus believes Papias to have been a disciple of St. John. Eusebius in his *Chronicle* agrees with St. Irenaeus and in his *Church History* adopts another opinion and asserts he was the disciple of the presbyter John, but Eusebius is probably wrong in his conclusion. Eusebius believed Papias to have been a man of mediocre talents and he ridicules him for his Chiliasm (the theory of a thousand years after the general resurrection when Christ will reign on earth), his acceptance of fable and his incapacity to grasp figurative language in the Apostolic writers. The fragments collected by Eusebius, and others quoted by Apollinaris, are all we have of the work of Papias.

31

THE SHEPHERD OF HERMAS

The Shepherd of Hermas' or the Apocalypse, Pastor *(Poimen)*, is the longest and most remarkable of the Apostolic writings. **Contents.** It contains five visions *(horaseis)* twelve Commands *(entolai)* and ten Similitudes *(parobolai)*. Hermas, or the angel who speaks to him, in the last vision seems to distinguish two parts, I, Visions (1-4) that the Church in the guise of a *matron* exhibits to the author, and II, Commands and Similitudes (5-end) expounded to Hermas by an angel of penance in the garb of a shepherd, and the prominence of the second source of the revelation gives the title to the work. The central idea is *exhortation to penance*, because of the impending coming of the Lord. One Remission is granted, though with difficulty, to those guilty of adultery or fornication. The rigour of the work is to be explained by the imminence of persecutions and of the *Parousia*.

pt. I. In these visions the matron (the Church) growing younger appears in Vis. 4 as a bride and in the instructions she gives shows a steady progress of penitential exhortation. Vis. 3 is the most important. It presents the Communion of Saints under the image of a great tower rising from the water and built of square and shining blocks. Those who have lost grace are represented by stones lying about which must be trimmed and polished before being put into the tower. pt. II The Commands and similitudes to which Vis. 5 is introductory are to realise and explain pt. I. Commands have for their object faith in one God (1), simplicity (2), truthfulness (3), chastity (4), patience (5), discernment (6), fear of the Lord (7), temperance (8) trust in God (9), and so on to 12. The Similitudes warn against worldliness, speak of chastity, fasting, penance, tribulation, etc. The tenth ends with these words:

'Through you the building of the tower has been interrupted; if you do not make haste to do good, the tower will be finished and you will remain without' (Sim. X.4.4.). The book is diffuse, circumstantial, apocalyptic in form.

Importance. *Dogmatic Interest* lies chiefly in its teaching on the possibility of forgiveness of mortal sins, notably adultery and apostasy (Vis. 3; Sim. 8-10). The Shepherd admits forgiveness of sins by penance (metanoian hamartion, Command 4,3,3) only during the period of grace announced by him – in future time there will be only one remission *(metanoia mia)* of sins through baptism (Commands 4,3,1-6). The way to penance still open, is long and difficult (Sim. 6-8). The Shepherd is the earliest witness to the *Stations* or degrees of penitential satisfaction (Sim. 5, 1, 2). Discussion of Penance in the early Church is necessary for understanding of this problem which centres on the question whether the Church was conscious of her power to forgive all sins and used that power. Hermas is important in this discussion and other points of interest in him are his exposition of the way of doing penance, his ethics, teaching on conjugal fidelity, justification, the angels and the Church. (See Cayré-Howitt ad loc.).

Origin. The Muratorian fragment (c. 200) declares:

'And very recently in our own times, in the city of Rome, Hermas wrote the Pastor, when his brother Pius, the bishop, sat upon the chair of the city of Rome'.

This rules out Origen's identification of Hermas with Hermas in Romans XVI, and the veracity of the reference to Pope Clement (Vis. 2:4). Pius I was Pope from 140-155. Hermas tells us he was of a Greek and probably Christian family, was brought to Rome and sold as a slave. He was freed, married and was successful in business but unfortunate in his family. He was untruthful himself, his wife was a gossip and his children denounced their parents during a persecution. It was in Rome, on the road from Rome to Cumae, that he received the revelations of the matron. The work was written about the middle of the second century as is obvious from the interest in forgiveness of sins and the fact that the first fervour has gone and it is necessary to renew ecclesiastical discipline. Circumstances that impelled Hermas to write were faults in his own past life and the faults of Christians and he wished to preach penance, its possibility and necessity. He was not a 'petit bourgeois', or a fiery reformer. He seems to have been a priest but not a man of great culture or depth of learning, but he was an excellent moralist and a close observer of the manners of his day, moderate in his demands, and made a clear distinction between obligations and counsels of perfection.

History. St. Irenaeus, Clement of Alexandria and Origen considered it inspired and ranked it with Scripture but were aware (Origen certainly) that the matter was disputed. Eusebius and St. Athanasius approved of it for catechumens. St. Jerome ridiculed some portions of it. Tertullian as a Catholic approved and as a Montanist denounced it ('*scriptura Pastoris quae solos moechos amat*', 'the book "Pastor" which values adulters only', etc.), as false and spurious. Interest in it gradually decreased,

33

after Tertullian's time, in the west, and had gone so much in St. Jerome's time that he could say of the book *'apud Latinos paene ignotus est'*, *'The Latins scarcely know of it'* (*De Vir. Illus.* c. 10).

II. THE APOLOGETIC LITERATURE OF THE SECOND CENTURY

Background. There was very serious State opposition to Christianity in the second century now that the State knew of its existence as distinct from Judaism, and this resulted in the Roman persecutions. Men of letters opposed Christianity vehemently too. An intellectual movement known as *Gnosticism* was one of the Church's greatest enemies. This was encouraged and supported by *Judaeo-Christians* and *Montanists*. The Christian life was a warfare and the majority of the writers are *apologists* or *controversialists*. Under the *Antonines* from Trajan to Commodus the Church suffered severely. Nero's law against Christians, though softened by Trajan's rescript *'conquirendi non sunt'*, 'They are not to be sought out', (Trajan ordered that Christians be punished when found but forbade officials to seek them out), was used as a threat and applied in the empire – there was constant popular *rioting*. Even under Antoninus Pius and the philosopher Marcus Aurelius there were Christian martyrs. *Writings* against the Church were mainly lost, all ordered to be burned c. 445 (by Emperor Theodosius), but the important names are *Fronto of Cirta* (d. 166?), the friend and preceptor of Antoninus; *Lucian of Samosata* (d. 190?), who wrote *De Morte Peregrini*, a satire on Christians and Cynics; and above all *Celsus*, a philosopher of distinction and culture who studied the Old and New Testament thoroughly to attack them effectively. His *True Word* has been reconstructed almost entirely from Origen's treatment. It has four parts: (1) A Jew shows how Christians have deformed the Messianic ideal; (2) A pagan shows the falsity of Jewish Messianism; (3) Celsus directly attacks Christian faith and morals; (4) he defends Paganism. Celsus was a formidable opponent – he is a politician as well as a scholar and concerned to have the religion of the country preserved. His lengthy attack is, in itself, clear proof that Christianity was, before the end of the second century, a power to contend with.

Judaeo-Christianity wanted to combine faith and Christianity with the Mosaic Law. A number of uncompromising converts from the Pharisees (*Acts* 15 etc.) maintained the absolute necessity of the observance of Judaism. Moderate followers invoked the authority of St. James the Less, did not dogmatise, but followed out the legal prescriptions of Judaism. A third body were more anxious about extra-legal observances, proper to the perfect, which they borrowed from various philosophical systems and religions – *syncretism* – (especially those subject to foreign influence).

'The Christians are opposed by the Jews as strangers, and are persecuted by the heathens' *(Letter to Diognetus)*. Calumnies of all kinds; violent outbreaks against them stimulated by pagan writers and leaders and priests and Jews; the official hostility of the State which saw itself and its authority clearly menaced – these Christianity faced daily and in these circumstances Apologetic literature arose. It is a defence, *apologia*, vindication, an attempt to meet attacks and rebut and refute them, to show the falsity of the accusations of *concubitus Oedipodei, epulae Thyesteae, (incest, ritual infanticide)*, political burden and social uselessness. That was the negative side. The positive side was the setting forth and proving the Christian religion as the only true religion, and the falsity of paganism and abolition of Judaism. Some apologies are against the heathens, some against the Jews. Only the amount necessary to refute calumny is set forth usually. As the writers often refer to the germs of truth in paganism they offer the first attempt at harmonising the teachings of reason and revelation. The writings against the Jews are fewer in number and less intent on refuting Jewish accusations than on the confirmation of Christians in their conviction that the Mosaic Law had only a temporary purpose and authority. The works are important and stylistically superior to the Apostolic writings. The authors were, as a rule, better educated than the first writers and were often *philosophers* and after their conversion put their philosophy at the service of their faith, Christianised their philosophy. Their initiative in this respect had tremendous consequences.

QUADRATUS. ARISTIDES OF ATHENS. ARISTO OF PELLA

Quadratus was a disciple of the Apostles, from Asia Minor. Eusebius records that on the occasion of a persecution of the Christians he presented an apology to Hadrian (117-138) – the earliest one we have – and the only fragment extant is in a citation in Eusebius. The date is c. 124, date of Hadrian's visit to Athens. Quadratus, bishop of Athens, is probably a different person.

Aristides of Athens is mentioned by Eusebius, after Quadratus, as having 'left an apology of the faith dedicated to Hadrian'. In 1878 a fragment of it was found, and in 1899 a complete Syriac translation was discovered by Rendel Harris in Sinai. A Greek revision a little later was found by A. Robinson. There is an Armenian translation also. They all show freedom in dealing with the original, as may be seen from chapters 1 and 2 of the fragment. It was presented to Antoninus Pius (138-161) most probably (not to Hadrian). Its aim is to prove that Christians alone possess the true knowledge of God. The author introduces himself as an 'Athenian philosopher' and develops a thesis based on the idea of God. Having set forth the idea of God eternal, impassible, perfect, as known from nature (c. 1) he invites the emperor to examine the faith in God shown by the four groups of mankind: Barbarians; Greeks (and Egyptians and Chaldees); Jews; Christians. (Christians alone have the correct idea and worthily worship God). Barbarians adore earth, water, fire, etc. (3-7); Greeks attribute their frailties to the god (8-13); Jews believe in one God but serve his angels rather (15). The Christians have the full truth and live it.

Conclusion (17). Cease to persecute Christians – be converted to their teaching. Ideas are: God, his nature; moral superiority of Christianity. There are echoes of biblical writings, the *Didache*, St. Peter's preaching. Celsus was acquainted with this Apology.

'Greece was the cradle of Christian Apologetics in the second century, and the genius of the Greeks set its mark on them'. (Bardenhewer.)

Aristo of Pella (a town of the Decapolis in Palestine), seems to have been the first to direct an apology against the Jews. His work was published between 135 and 175 – A *Discussion Between Jason and Papiscus Concerning Christ*. Jason, a Jewish Christian, proves so conclusively that the Messianic prophecies are fulfilled in Jesus that the Jew, Papiscus, begs to be baptized. The work is lost. A fragment of it in St. Jerome shows that the Jews objected to the Christians that Christ died on a cross – 'scandalum crucis'. There are traces of it in Origen, and Celsus knew and despised it as a tissue of absurdities.

37

ST. JUSTIN MARTYR

St. Justin Martyr is one of the most important of these writers. Tertullian called him 'philosophus et martyr'. He was 'the son of Priscus – of Flavia Neapolis' i.e. Nablus or Naplouse (the ancient Sichem) in Palestine, about the first decade of the second century. His parents were pagan. He studied in different schools of philosophy, Stoic, Peripatetic, Pythagorian, and Platonic and after a long stay with the Platonists found in Christianity the object of his search, A.D. 130-135. At Ephesus or Caesarea of Palestine he was shown by an old man how much was wanting in philosophy, was directed to the Bible and was soon convinced 'that this Christian philosophy alone was sure and profitable'. He remained a philosopher, wore the philosopher's mantle and defended Christianity by his knowledge of philosophy in writings and in speech. Twice he came to Rome and there opened, as other philosophers did, a school in which to teach his philosophy – Christianity – (something like the great catechetical school of Alexandria). Probably while there (c. 152) he sent to the emperor the famous *Plea in favour of the Christians'* beginning:

'To the Emperor... Antoninus Pius... and to Verissimus (Marcus Aurelius) his son, philosopher... to the Roman Senate and to all the Roman people, in favour of all men of all races who are unjustly hated and persecuted, Justin, son of Priscus, *one from among them*, addresses this discourse and plea'.

A few years later, he wrote a *second apology* inspired by the hopes created by the personality of the Emperor-philosopher (his influence was felt even before the end of Antoninus's reign – (132-161). A Christian woman separated herself from a profligate husband who denounced Ptolemy (his wife's catechist), and Urbicus, the Prefect of Rome, had him arrested and executed with two of his companions. Exasperated by this, Justin protested again. In this he accuses (c. 3) the Cynic philosopher, Crescens, of immorality and ignorance and earned his undying hostility. Probably this Crescens denounced Justin and caused him to be martyred, c.A.D. 165 (with six others). 'The warmth of St. Justin's convictions, the nobility of his character, and the perfect straightforwardness of his behaviour have always been a subject of admiration'. (Tixeront.)

Writings. Two Apologies; Dialogue with Tryphon; *On the Resurrection* (only fragments remain). These are the only authentic remaining works of St. Justin. He is reputed the author of a vast number of treatises. He is the most outstanding writer in this group, opposing heathen, Jew and heretic alike.

Apologies. I. In the Paris Codex (A.D. 1364) the two apologies are found. The first possibly conforms to rhetorical rules of prooemium, propositio (of the charge against Christians); refutatio; probatio; peroratio, (salutation, statement, refutation, proof, peroration). It is by far the longer and more orderly of the two. The first part (cc. 4-13) is negative and refutes the anti-Christian calumnies of impiety and civil enmity. Second part (14-67) – a positive exposition and justification of the contents of Christianity – maintains that Christ, founder of the doctrine and system, is the Son of God as He is the fulfilment of the Jewish prophecies. In conclusion (68) he appeals to the imperial sense of justice for justice for the Christians. Date – about 150-155 (see above).

II. The *second* is shorter and owes its origin to events described above. These events are related, 'apologetic' paragraphs added and a plea; the apology calls on the emperor to publish the first apology and to command that justice be observed in dealings with the Christians. It is a supplement to the first and has no dominant idea and little order. Date – between 140 and 160.

Dialogue with Trypho. This work has reached us in an imperfect state in the same Paris Codex. It lacks the introduction, dedication and a great part of c. 74. It is a summary of a disputation held at Ephesus (A.D. 132-135) between Justin and the Jew Trypho, extending over two days. According to Zahn there is a mixture of truth and fiction – in part real discussions between Justin and learned Jews, and in part an original study. Trypho may well be the celebrated contemporary Rabbi Tarpho. In the introduction (2-8) Justin describes the development of his own religious opinions; Part I (10-47) proves from the Old Testament that the ritual Law of Moses has been abrogated in favour of the new Law of Christ; Part II proves (48-108) that the adoration of Jesus does not conflict with Jewish Monotheism. Part III (109-141) shows that the true Israel is to be found in all those who have accepted Christianity. Date is A.D. 150-155.

Lost Works are known to us (their names, and fragments). The *Sacra Parallela* of St. John Damascene has three long portions of *De Resurrectione*, which refutes Gnostic objections to the resurrection of the body. Besides smaller works, we have, from Eusebius, the names of (a) *Discourse Against the Greeks*, an examination of 'the matters that are treated by us and by the Greek philosophers'; (b) A *Refutation*, against the Greeks also; (c) *On the Unity of God*, based on Christian and Greek writings; (d) Psalter. The titles of the first three are identical with those of three works preserved in the MSS. of St. Justin *(Cohortatio ad Gentiles, De Monarchia, Oratio ad Gentiles)* which cannot be ascribed to him because of differences of style, etc.

Spurious Writings. Apart from the last three mentioned, many works are falsely attributed to him. Because of his style and method there has been more difficulty in deciding on his authentic works than in the case of any other early writer. *Epistle to Diognetus; Expositio fidei seu De Trinitate, Epistola ad Zenam et Serenum,* and others.

Authentic Works. St. Justin is not a careful, logical writer. He is an impressionist, jotting down certain points and without waiting to develop them, hurrying on to other ideas. There are ideas with little affinity, little beauty of diction, solecisms, neologisms, long and involved periods and constructions, and sometimes great monotony, with periods of great life and power and emotion and even sublimity. He was the first and one of the most eminent of the Fathers who essayed the reconciliation of pagan science and Christianity. Some modern writers (e.g. Aube) find more Platonism than Christianity, but this is untrue. For Justin Christianity is the rule by which he measures the data of philosophy and in it he saw the fullness of truth. He taught that whatever good or truth was in Greek philosophy was borrowed from the Old Testament – Plato's moral freedom is borrowed from Moses, e.g., also the immortality of the soul, future retribution, heaven, etc. He outlines the relation between pagan culture and Christianity. He gives, also, an account of *Christian liturgy* (Apol. I, 61 ff.) which is very important, as he goes beyond the limits of the Discipline of the Secret and describes in detail the rites connected with Baptism and the Eucharist. No other apologist has made such a disclosure of the Christian mysteries.

Tatian the Assyrian born in Assyria about A.D. 120, belongs to the Syrian race. He was one of St. Justin's disciples and belonged to the Roman community until Justin's death. He received a Greek education, was scholarly and cultured, a philosopher and writer, and travelled as a Sophist from town to town lecturing. He was initiated into several mysteries and finally became a convert to Christianity (c. 165). He attended

St. Justin's course in Rome, and eventually opened a school himself. About 172 he left the Church and joined the Gnostic Encratites and returned to the East (Antioch, Cilicia, and Pisidia). He forbade marriage; believed in a series of aeons. Clement of Alexandria refuted him in his *Stromata*. Tatian died in the East – date unknown.

Works. (1) *The Apology* is the only work that has survived – *Oratio ad Graecos (Pros hEllenas)* – an Apology for Christianity, or rather a criticism of Hellenis,. (a) 1-4. Refutation of Greek prejudices; (b) 4-31. argument for Christianity from its sublime doctrine; (c) 31. argument from its antiquity. He outlines in (b) the teaching on God, the world, sin redemption, and satirises the errors of the Greeks in these matters, and in 22-29 indulges in polemics. In (c) he points out that Homer, at the beginning of Greek civilisation, is four hundred years later than Moses. In direct contrast to St. Justin he belittles and insults the thinkers and poets of Greece, abounds in denunciation, and ignores all the praiseworthy features of the Greek culture. The *purpose* of his apology is to justify his conversion, after which he probably published it, c. 165. The influence of *Stoicism* is marked, and many phrases can be interpreted as contrary to the teaching of the Church. He teaches clearly that Christ is God (c. 13, 21). In one passage on the Word he teaches subordinationism (of the Son to the Father).

(2) The *Diatesseron*, a *Gospel-harmony (To Dia Tessaron Euangelion)* is extant in fragments only. It is important as a witness to the authority of the four canonical Gospels. Tatian composed it after his apostasy, probably not in Greek but in Syriac. Throughout the third century this 'harmony' was the only Gospel text used in many places in Syria and only after the middle of the fourth century the 'Gospel of the Mixed' gave way to the 'Gospel of the Separated'. Between 360 and 370 St. Ephraem the Syrian wrote a commentary on the *Diatessaron*. Theodoret of Cyrus (d. 458) removed more than 200 copies of this work from churches in his diocese and he put there the Syriac version of the Four Gospels. The *Diatessaron* can be partially reconstructed from St. Ephraem's commentary (an Armenian version). In character Tatian resembles Tertullian more than St. Justin. He goes to excess, mocks, is violent; aims less at apology than at attacking Graeco-Roman culture. 'He had nothing good to say of the pagans; the art of the Greeks is immoral, their literature is puerile, their philosophy mendacious, and even their language is neither consistent nor pure'

(Tixeront). He has many faults himself. He is harsh and passionate, employs a style often rough and disjointed, and often affected. As a satirist, however, he is biting and animated. He is a clever writer, and occasionally rises to poetic heights by the very vigour of thought and conviction. There are many other works – e.g. *On Animals* – all have been lost.

MILTIADES. APOLLINARIS OF HIERAPOLIS. MELITO OF SARDIS. ATHENAGORAS OF ATHENS

Miltiades of Asia Minor was a contemporary of Tatian and defended Christian truth against heathens, heretics and Jews. All his works have been lost.

Apollinaris, Bishop of Hierapolis, in the reign of M. Aurelius, left a number of works which Eusebius mentions – all lost. c. 172.

Melito, bishop of Sardis in Lydia (Asia Minor), left extensive and varied works. Eusebius was acquainted with a long list of them. Pope Victor (189-199) names him among the 'great luminaries' of Asia now dead. About A.D. 170 he addressed to Marcus Aurelius an apology for the Christians; fragments of it are preserved in Eusebius's *Church History* and in it is a sentence important for author's ideal of Church-State relations. 'He is the first to advocate solidarity of Christianity with the empire' (Quasten). A recent interesting find is Melito's *Homily on the Passion* (nearly complete) which Campbell Bonner discovered and published. The *Homily* takes up the latter part of a codex (4th century), eight leaves of which belong to the collection of Sir Alfred Chester Beatty and the British Museum, six to the University of Michigan. It is a Good Friday sermon.

Athenagoras of Athens is called in the title to his work the 'Christian philosopher of Athens'. According to tradition he was from Alexandria and presented an Apology to Hadrian and Antoninus (Pius) and was the first master of the catechetical school of Alexandria. The introduction to the Apology shows it was addressed to Marcus Aurelius and Commodus, and probably in A.D. 177. The purpose is the usual one – to show the falsity and absurdity of the current calumnies – atheism, immorality, etc. (c. 3). Atheism is refuted by an exposition of the Christian doctrine concerning God (4-30); the other charges are met by setting forth the principles of Christian morality. The title is *Supplication for the Christians*. Minucius

Felix (possibly) and Methodius of Olympus show acquaintance with the work. A second work, *On the Resurrection of the Dead (Peri Anastaseos Nekron)*, is in two parts: (1) objections refuted; (2) reality of it proved (a) from the eternal destiny of man; (b) retribution necessary for body and soul; (c) the last end of man as unattainable in this life (c. 24-25).

Characteristics. Bossuet terms him 'the author of one of the finest and earliest apologies of the Christian religion'. He is little known, but is an attractive stylist, less original than Justin and Tatian, but superior to them in 'felicity of expression purity and beauty of diction, simplicity and lucidity of arrangement'. He knew and respected the Greek classics, especially Platonic philosophy. His selection of Christian doctrines to rebut calumny is admirable. His rational proof of the unity of God is the first scientific attempt of Christians to justify their Monotheism, and his witness to the Blessed Trinity is in terms of great clearness and precision (c. 10).

ST. THEOPHILUS OF ANTIOCH. THE LETTER TO DIOGNETUS. HERMIAS THE PHILOSOPHER

St. Theophilus of Antioch was seventh bishop of Antioch (169-180), not a philosopher apologist, but a man of letters. He possessed an easy and elegant style, and was a writer with personal and original ideas. He was born near the Euphrates, and was of mature age when converted, received a Greek education and had a knowledge of Hebrew. He wrote on many subjects. We have his *Discourse to Autolycus* (3 books). He composed works (now lost) on the origins of mankind (according to the Bible and mythology); controversial writings; pastoral writings; commentaries on the Bible, of which only fragments quoted by St. Jerome remain. In the *Discourse to Autolycus*, Book I treats of the faith of Christians in an invisible God (2-11), and of the name 'Christian'. Book II discusses the folly of the heathen idolatry, and sets forth the teaching of the prophets of God. Book III is a repudiation of anti-Christian calumnies, and asserts that the Sacred Scriptures are more ancient than Greek history and literature.

The Letter to Diognetus is frequently ascribed to St. Justin, and answers questions asked by a heathen interested in Christianity – the exact nature of Christian worship, and how it differs from pagan and Jewish worship, the change it brings about in Christian life (especially love of our neighbour) and why Christianity appeared only now, and not earlier. 'The replies to these questions are distinguished for elevation of tone, profound grasp of the Christian ideas, magnificence and splendour of exposition. The portrait of the daily life of the Christians (5-6) is positively fascinating' (Bardenhewer). Its qualities of style and clarity and method make it most unlikely to be St. Justin's work. The author is unknown – Marcion, Apelles, Aristides of Athens are mentioned but are unlikely. Quadratus has been mentioned recently. The work was written during the persecution. 'The expistle deserves to rank among the most brilliant and beautiful works of Christian-Greek literature. The writer is a master of rhetoric, his sentence structure is full of charm and subtly balanced, his style limpid. The diction sparkles with fire and vitality' (Quasten).

Hermias the Philosopher wrote *Irrisio gentilium philosophorum (Diasurmos ton exo Philosophon)*. The work satirises contradictory opinions of Greek philosophers concerning the human soul (1-2), and the universe (3-10). It is able and witty but superficial. It is not mentioned in Christian antiquity, but certainly belongs to the period of conflict between Christianity and Hellenic philosophy.

MINUCIUS FELIX

Minucius Felix is the author of *Octavius*, possibly, the earliest Christian literary work in *Latin*. Renan terms it 'the pearl of apologetical literature' (Marc-Aurèle, p. 389). It is in the form of a dialogue between the Christian Octavius Januarius and the pagan Caecilus Natalis, both friends of the author, Minucius Felix, a Roman lawyer. (A) 1-4. Introduction; (B) 5-13. Defence of paganism; (C) 14-38. The victorious answer of Octavius. Cc. 39-41. relate the conversion of Caecilius. (*A*) The three friends are at Ostia on holidays, their work at the law-courts being finished. A discussion arises, and Minucius promises to act as arbiter. (*B*) Caecilius pleads the cause of paganism, and though a sceptic himself, asserts that the Roman religion, as a beneficent national institution and the source of Roman greatness, must be maintained. The Christians are unwise in attacking it, and are far from irreproachable themselves. He then advances all the usual charges – their impiety, criminal association, immorality, infanticide, their revolting doctrines of a crucified God, and foolish belief in the resurrection. (*C*) Octavius refutes these calumnies, establishes the existence and unity of God, the unreasonableness of polytheism, which is the work of the devil, and gives a moving description of Christian life. He concludes: '*cohibeatur superstitio, impietas expietur, vera religio reservetur*', *(superstition should be suppressed, irreligion atoned for, and true religion upheld)*. Caecilius admits defeat, and seeks further information before becoming a Christian.

None of the second or third century Christian apologies can compare with *Octavius* for artistic composition and treatment of the theme. The method is entirely classical, and the best standard of Latin prose is maintained in the purity and harmony of the language. The author models himself on Cicero's *De natura deorum* and uses *De divinatione*, also Seneca's *De providentia* and *De superstitione*. He does not quote them, but expressions and mannerisms from them are everywhere evident. There is a generous humanitarian tone throughout. He insists on Christian monotheism, and Christian practical morality. There is little enough space given to Christian dogma, but the purpose in view was to give Roman society an apology of Christianity suitable to its refined literary taste, and the book was meant to be an introduction, not a catechism. The author makes no mention of the Christian mysteries, nor does he quote the Scriptures.

Author and Date. St. Jerome and Lactantius give his full name. He was probably African by birth, and a lawyer, in Rome, by profession. He was converted fairly late in life. For many years his work was considered later than Tertullian's *Apologeticum*, which it resembles closely (it was written in A.D. 197), and indebted to it (Massebieau, Harnack, Monceaux). Bardenhewer believes, with Ebert, etc., that it was Tertullian made use of Minucius's work. Fronto of Cirta (died c. 175) must have been alive, or a well-known name, when *Octavius* was composed (c. 9, 6; 31, 2). St. Cyprian's work *Quod idola dii non sint* (c. 248) uses *Octavius* freely. *Octavius* may have been written at the beginning of Commodus's reign (180-192).

III. HERETICAL LITERATURE OF THE SECOND CENTURY, AND NEW TESTAMENT APOCRYPHA

The apologies were occasioned by the conflict between paganism and Christianity. Heresy proved an even more dangerous enemy, constituting a threat not against the existence but the purity and integrity of Christianity. There were heresies from the very beginning.

Gnosticism was the most influential of the early heresies. The term is generic and embraces a great variety of teachings. Based on the theory of a dual principle, it rejected creation, made great headway in the East and West, and produced a rich and varied literature. With the exception of a few works in Coptic this literature has perished, and is known to us only in fragments quoted by the ecclesiastical writers.

History. The chief names are Basilides and Isidorus (120-140) the *Ophites* (Brethren of the Serpent); Carpocratians; Valentine and followers; Bardesanes, and Harmonius; Marcion and Apelles. At the time of the appearance of Christianity, in the Roman empire moral and religious feelings were in a state of ferment. Religious aspirations, dissatisfied with official religion, turned anxiously to the exotic Eastern religions and to Greek philosophy, both of which the Roman conquests had made known. Every charlatan from the East was welcomed and, in spite of State laws, the cults of Isis and Osiris, Mithra, etc. spread between 100 B.C. and 100 A.D., pandering to the craving for novelty. Into this general ferment were thrown Jewish monotheism and Christianity, and by some they were eagerly welcomed, even if only temporarily. But (leaving aside the question of Judaism) Christianity was a radical condemnation of all the other religions and its appeal was limited. People sought to transform it into a religious philosophy, or tried to give the religious mysteries a philosophical explanation. *Gnosis* (knowledge) takes the place of faith and is a form of knowledge not vouchsafed to the ordinary mortal. In the third century an orthodox gnosis sought to expound the mysteries philosophically in conformity with faith, but the in the second century it is a heretical gnosis supplanting revelation.

Starting-point was good (1) exalted idea of God, infinite, remote from material nature, the Great Silence *(sigé)* and

46

Depth *(bythos)*. (2) inferiority of matter, which is considered evil because it turns men from God. How then could God create matter? Whence the origin of the world of matter, and the origin of evil? The Gnostics found the Christian answer (creation from nothing; and evil, a negation of good, due to man's free will) too simple and elaborated several solutions which have one common feature – the existence of an *intermediary series* which bridges the gulf between God and creation. The doctrines of Gnosticism (a system of gnosis) are quite unacceptable to a Christian and were really suited only to Eastern religions; they emanated from Ephesus in Proconsular Asia.

Doctrines. The attempt to retain and explain Christianity in terms of exotic cults and eclectic philosophy did not easily attain the proportions of a harmonious whole. God's unity could not be successfully maintained if evil were to be explained as something positive, so God was distinguished from the *Demiurge*, Maker of the World, and there was a hierarchy of *Aeons* or inferior gods. (1) There is one God, separate from matter. (2) The aeons are intermediary between God and matter (eternal), the first *syzygy*, (a couple, male and female), being produced by God himself directly, and it produced a second – the complete series of aeons being the Pleroma. As they recede from God the aeons become less perfect, one finally goes astray, is cast out into a lower world and peoples it with fresh aeons, and the declension in good continues. This rejected aeon finally creates and the material world – it is the *Demiurge*, the God of the Jews and of evil.

(3) *Man* is not entirely corrupt. A divine seed or spark detached from the higher world by the higher aeons was introduced into matter where the Demiurge kept it prisoner and persecuted it. Men are either (a) *pneumatikoi*, i.e. influenced by the spirit, Gnostics, in possession of the divine element and certain of salvation; or (b) *psychikoi*, psychicists – could be saved by gnosis; or (c) *hylikoi* – these under influence of matter and without hope of salvation. (4) *Redemption* aims at delivering the divine spark in matter. One of the first aeons was accidentally united with Jesus from his baptism to his passion and had human nature (Docetism). It was a man suffered and the quasi-divine Being had no part in the Redemption in our sense. Salvation was not obtained through Jesus's merits, but through the Gnosis manifested in him. (5) After the redemption of the divine element and the submission of the Demiurge the *universal restoration* will be attained, the material world

47

destroyed with the men not destined to salvation.

Moral teaching. Once a man had the Gnosis he was assured of salvation and he could do as he pleased. Some, however, taught that the body was to be despised and subjected but the majority held that it could be enjoyed with impunity. Results were to be seen in *Encratite* school, e.g. which held that marriage was unlawful because of procreation and *Antionomians* who held that all government comes from the Demiurge, is tyranny and should be overthrown.

We are indebted to St. Irenaeus, the *Philosophumena*, (Hippolytus) and St. Epiphanius for our knowledge of Gnosticism. There were three main groups: (A) Syrian; (B) Alexandrian; (C) Valentinian.

(A) Names – Simon Magus, Cerinthus; Menander; Saturninus.

(B) Basilides brought a Gnosis-teaching from Antioch; his son Isidorus, and Carpocrates 'who reduced immortality to a system'; Valentinus (v. *infra*); Cainites; Sethians; Ophites; (these sects were responsible for a lot of literature, cf. *Pistis-Sophia*, published 1851).

(C) Valentinus carried on Basilides's work in Egypt and in Rome (135-160), where he was excommunicated more than once. He went to Cyprus, and lost the faith there. The western writers taught a modified, the eastern writers pure Docetism.

Marcionism is a tempered form of Gnosticism. Authors: *Cerdo*, who came to Rome as disciple of Valentinus and *Marcion*, son of the bishop of Sinope, in Pontus, who cast him out of the Church. He came to Rome c. 135 and gave much money to the poor and was received into the Church and soon cast out again for teaching heresy. His teaching is Gnostic, as in his work *Antitheses* – a collection of alleged contradictions in New and Old Testament texts. He rejected the Old Testament as the work of a rigidly just, cruel and vindictive God. He taught the New Dispensation as the work of a good God and asserts it is being corrupted by Jewish efforts. Gnostic dualism and Docetism he retains along with a rigid moral teaching. His teaching was formidable, successful; and the title 'Wolf of Pontus' given by Tertullian he well merited for the harm he did the Christian flock. A separate Church organised by him survived until the fifth century. The chief writer of the sect was *Apelles*.

Montanism opposed the *authority* of the Christian hierarchy directly by its profession of prophecy (Gnosticism had opposed the *teaching* of the hierarchy with its own teaching). It developed in Phrygia especially, in the second century, and in Carthage in the third. In the second century the *charisms* had practically disappeared. The Phrygian, *Montanus*, feigned to restore them. Shortly after his baptism he began to prophesy (c. 156 or 172) but convulsions and ecstasies attended his prophecies. He announced himself as the organ of the Holy Ghost – the fulfilment of 'I will send you a Paraclete', and his prophecies and revelations were to supersede Christ's revelation. He attracted many followers especially *Maximilla* and *Priscilla*, who left their husbands, claimed they had visions and became leaders. The Montanists wished to remain in the Church as a more perfect group but the Phrygian bishops resisted them and in 177 the Church of Lyons was disturbed by them and wrote to Rome (St. Eleutherius) and the Churches of Asia about them. At the beginning of the third century they set up separate communities. They taught the imminence of the Second Coming and Christ's reign for a thousand years. *Moral teaching* was austere and set aside allowance Christ made for the flesh. (1) Second marriages were forbidden (and first marriages at the beginning); (2) more fasts; (3) sins committed after baptism were not forgiven. The followers were either *Spirituals* or *Psychicists*. The *chute lamentable* of Tertullian is one of the chief reasons for their importance. They split up into several *sects*, Montanists according to Proclus, to Aeschines etc., and the most celebrated sect was the Tertullianists.

Apocrypha of the New Testament were written by various heretics to bolster up their position, and serve chiefly to throw into relief the genuine, dispassionate, completely authentic note of, and ring about the canonical books. They often enshrine current tradition, of course, are often interesting, sometimes dull. Apocryphal-Gospels; Acts of the Apostles; Letters of the Apostles; Apocalypses; Gospel according to the Hebrews; of the Twelve; of the Egyptians; of Peter; Matthias; Philip; Thomas; Andrew; Barnabas; Bartholomew; Proto-evangelium of James; Acta Pilati; Preaching of Peter and Paul; Acts of Peter; Paul; Peter and Paul; Paul and Thecla; Andrew; John; Thomas; Philip; Matthew; Legend of Thaddaeus; Letter to the Laodiceans (St. Paul); to the Alexandrines (Paul and Marcion); Corinthians (pseu. 3rd letter of St. Paul); Correspondence between St. Paul and Seneca (eight short letters of Seneca and six shorter replies of St. Paul –

poor in diction and style – mentioned by St. Jerome. The legend of Seneca's conversion, on which these letters are based, owes its origin to the ethico-theistic character of Seneca's writings); Apocalypse of Peter; Paul.

Judaistic Literature. *Ebionites, Elkesaites* (both had writings); *Clementine Literature* (treating of St. Clement's life and purporting to come from him). For detailed information on Apocryphal literature see Bardenhewer, *Patrology*, pp. 85-116; Cayré-Howitt, *Manual of Patrology*, pp. 156-165.

IV. ANTI-HERETICAL LITERATURE OF
THE SECOND CENTURY

Anti-Gnostics. Some lost works. The Church to refute heretics had to prove herself the sole custodian of the truth, to oppose especially the teachings of the Gnostics on the unity of God, redemption, and to discuss the sources and criteria of the teachings of the Church. This literature greatly surpassed the apologetic writings as a propaedeutic and a foundation for theology.

Many authors were apologists as well as controversialists. *St. Justin* wrote against all heresies and Marcion in particular; *St. Theophilus* attacked Gnosticism; *Miltiades* refuted Montanists and Gnostics; *Apollinaris* of Hierapolis; *Melito* of Sardis – works all lost except fragments (see above).

Adversaries of Montanism. (a) An *anonymous* author in Phrygia – his books gave the Montanist teaching and Eusebius relied on it (192-200). (b) *Apollonius*, bishop of Ephesus (?). (c) Caius, a Roman priest under Pope Zephyrinus (199-217) – to refute Montanism all the better he rejected St. John's Gospel, but he was probably in good faith and was not condemned.

Adversaries of Gnosticism.

(a) *Rhodo*, one of Tatian's disciples in Rome.

(b) *Hegesippus* (110?-180?) – a Jew born in Syria or Palestine and converted to Christianity. He visited various Churches and came to Rome in the time of Pope Anicetus (c. 155-166) and survived Pope Eleutherius (174-179) possibly. He returned home (174-179) and compiled his *Memoirs (hypomnemata)* from notes taken on his travels. He died under Commodus (180-192). The fragments in Eusebius are historical in character, but St. Jerome is probably in error when he reckons him as the first Church historian. More probably the work was a polemical writing aiming at proving the official Church teaching against the Gnostics. He insists on the uninterrupted succession of bishops as a guarantee of apostolicity of their doctrine. He drew up a list of the Jewish and first Gnostic sects. He was mediocre, perspicacious as an observer, and a good, reliable witness to tradition.

Others: *Philippus* of Gorstyna; *Modestus*; *Modenus*; *Heraclitus*.

✓ ST. IRENAEUS OF LYONS

St. Irenaeus of Lyons is the great figure of this period. The first historical mention of him is in A.D. 177 when he was a priest in Lyons, St. Pothinus being bishop there. The persecution of Marcus Aurelius was in force and the clergy of Lyons and Vienne, many of them in prison, sent Irenaeus to Pope Eleutherius in Rome with a letter on Montanist troubles in Lyons. On his return he was made bishop in succession to the martyred Pothinus and he devoted his energies to the overthrow of the false Gnosis. He was a native of Asia Minor and probably from Smyrna, born about A.D. 140. He says himself that he listened as a child to the discourses of Polycarp. He is said to have been in Rome when Polycarp died (155). Attachment to tradition, love and knowledge of the Scriptures, depth of faith and breadth of knowledge, a liberal education, and enquiring mind combined to make him one of the great Church Fathers. Tertullian calls him 'a curious explorer of all doctrines'. Besides his struggle against Gnosticism, he strove to spread Christianity in the provinces adjacent to Lyons. We know that he intervened in the Easter Controversy about 190. The Church in Asia Minor held Easter on the 14th of Nisan; Jews did likewise; Rome celebrated it on the following Sunday. Pope Victor tried to have the matter ended and all obeyed except the Asian prelates and Polycrates of Ephesus, who held on to their Apostolic tradition, and Victor wished to excommunicate them. Irenaeus intervened in their favour. Before his death Irenaeus witnessed the looting and partial destruction of Lyons in 197. Tradition fixes his death 202-203 and St. Jerome (alone) says he was martyred. In 1562 the Calvinists scattered his remains and only his head has been found.

Works. Two complete treatises (*The Proof*, *Adversus Haereses*) and some fragments are his extant writings. *The Proof of the Apostolic Preaching* is a non-controversial summary of Christian teaching.

Adversus Haereses (five books) is his main work 'Detection and Overthrow of the pretended but false Gnosis', (Elenchos kai anatropé tes pseudonomou gnoseos). We have only a Latin translation of the Greek, literal to the point of slavishness, and fragments of the Greek in citations of other authors and in a Syriac translation. It was begun at the request of a friend (a bishop?) and was intended to be brief but it expanded. Its composition extended over a long period. In Book III Eleutherius is mentioned as the contemporary bishop of Rome. The result of the long time and change of purpose is that there is lack of method, and lack of consecutiveness of thought, as well as of progressive exposition.

Book I is the detection or exposition of errors, and II to V their refutation, and the exposition of the true doctrine; Book II gives arguments from reason and philosophy; III from Scripture and tradition; IV Scripture and tradition; V Defends the resurrection of the body, and sets forth his Chiliastic theories (millenium). The exposition of the true doctrine (III-V, to show its superiority over Gnosticism) is most important for the development of theology and has merited for the author the title of *Father of Catholic Theology*. He is the first to give such an exposition. The others were mainly concerned with one point; he gives the fundamental doctrines of Christianity, though not scientifically or methodically. Gnosticism denied almost everything, was the first serious heresy and brought home to Christians the menace heresy was likely to be, so that it became essential to have some test to enable one to know heresy readily. The early Christians had not felt the need for such, and had not a clear idea of it, but St. Irenaeus developed the manner of testing falsity. Dufourcq sums up his achievement in two phrases: 'he killed Gnosticism and founded Christian theology'. The heresy revived for a time in the third and fourth centuries but it had received a mortal blow from St. Irenaeus.

His Theology. (A) *Rule of Faith*. (Book III, 1-3 especially). Interpretation of Scripture, a source of faith, requires a 'fixed rule of faith', this rule being the baptismal symbolum or creed taught by the Church. The duty of fixing the form of the creed and explaining it belongs to the Church, which is aided and guided by the Holy Ghost – *'ubi enim ecclesia, ibi est Spiritus Dei'*, *('where the Church is, there is the Spirit of God')* etc. The true teaching of the Church is that handed down by the Apostles and held from them by unbroken tradition and succession. It is that of the mother-churches that can trace their bishops back to the beginning. The rule of faith is the present living magisterium of the Church. But, as a search of all these churches may be difficult, he tells us that there is a last criterion which is in the reach of everyone and is sufficient – it is the teaching of the Church of Rome. What agrees with Rome's teaching is correct, and this, though not the only, is the more compendious test. It is sufficient he says (III, iii, 2), to prove that 'the greatest and oldest Church, the one well-known to all men, founded and established at Rome by the two most glorious Apostles, Peter and Paul', can trace its bishops back to the Apostles; its teaching can rightly lay claim to apostolicity. 'Ad hanc enim ecclesiam propter potentiorem (potiorem) principalitatem necesse est omnem convenire ecclesiam, hoc est eos qui sunt undique fideles, in qua semper ab his qui sunt undique conservata est ea, quae est ab apostolis traditio', i.e. 'with this Church, because of its higher rank, every Church must agree, i.e. the faithful of all places, in which (in communion with which) the apostolic tradition has been always preserved by the (faithful) of all places' ('and it is in her – in qua, Rome, by communion with her) that the faithful of all countries have conserved the Apostolic tradition' – or, with Duchesne etc. refer 'in qua' to the Church 'per orbem' – each Church in which – in qua – the Ap. tradition is maintained, must be in accord with Rome. In either translation the value of the phrase is not lost).

Irenaeus states that the teaching of the Apostles continues on unaltered, and this tradition is the source and norm of faith. Only the churches founded by apostles can give authentic witness to the correct teaching and it is the succession of bishops in those churches that guarantees the truth of their doctrine. We can point out, he said, those who were made bishops in those churches by apostles and their successors, down to the present day. Heretics are not successors of the apostles and have not the charism of truth. But it would take very long to enumerate the episcopal lists in all the churches; so by giving the tradition that has come down in the greatest church of all – Rome – we refute those who are unauthorised, 'for with this church, because of its more efficient leadership, all churches must agree, i.e. to say, the faithful of all places; because in it the apostolic tradition has always been preserved by the faithful of all places'.

Most probably 'must agree' does not refer to moral obligation but to a fact, and the context suggests this. Irenaeus wants to show that the Gnostic claim to a special knowledge (not given to the apostles or to the general body but revealed only to the perfect) is foreign to the whole apostolic tradition. So this passage will not refer to ecclesiastical constitution, but to the faith common to the churches. The primacy of Rome is the reason why her faith is to be consulted; she has a 'potior principalitas', and her doctrine is conclusive proof of Christian faith.

(1) *The doctrinal unity of the Church*, and (2) unique *importance* and pre-eminence of the *Roman Church* as witness, guardian, and organ of apostolic tradition are very clearly taught.

(B) *Trinity* and *Unity* of God are explicitly set forth.

(C) *Christology*. He was attached to the doctrine of *recapitulation (anakephalaiosis)*. Man is free, sinned in Adam, his head. Jesus Christ, the new Adam, recapitulates in Himself all mankind and reconciles it with His Father, and is God, true man, the revealer of the last Testament, the redeemer, the sanctifier. The fruits of redemption, applied in baptism and the Eucharist, will be fully realised in the next life.

(D) *Mariology* and (E) *Christian* Spirituality are important points of his teaching too. (F.) *Eschatology* – it is 'a mixture of interesting ideas, of affirmations containing the substance of Christ's teaching, and of contestable or even frankly erroneous theories' (Vernet). He admitted the (heretical) opinion of the postponement, of the Beatific Vision until the General Judgment and believed that Christ would reign for 1,000 years with the just arisen from the grave.

Other Works (fragments only). (1) On the Monarchy or How God is not the cause of evil; (2) On the Ogdoad; (3) Treatise on Schism; (4) Letter to Pope Victor; (5) On the Subject of Knowledge; (6) Divers discourses.

Synods etc. Besides the efforts of individual writers Popes in synods dealt with heresy. Pope Soter (166-174) wrote a letter to Corinthians in the name of the Roman community. During the Easter controversy Pope Victor (189-199) wrote several letters, urging holding of synods, a letter promulgating the synodal decrees, and also some theological treatises. He was a native of Roman Africa.

Dionysius of Corinth, bishop, contemporary of Pope Soter, wrote (Eusebius) seven 'Catholic' epistles (and a private letter) to seven communities, Rome included.

V. ECCLESIASTICAL LITERATURE DURING THE GENESIS OF CHRISTIAN THEOLOGY

Background. Conditions in the third century were vastly different from those of the second. Trajan's 'conquirendi non sunt' was abrogated, and persecution by edict began. There were truces in this war on Christianity, when emperors were generous or simply indifferent. Notable persecutions were those of Septimius Severus after 202, Maximin the Thracian (235-238), and Decius and Valerian (249-260). In the periods of peace – about seventy-five years – the Church had an opportunity of organising and spreading. Efforts to renew declining paganism backed up the State persecutions.

Oriental Religions. *Religious syncretism* was favoured by many empresses, Julia Domna (wife of Septimius Severus) and Julia Mammaea (mother of Alexander Severus) being especially active. The Sun was chosen as the new god, and Apollonius of Tyana was proclaimed his prophet. *Mithraism* appears to have supplanted all other religions in the middle of the third century and the Roman soldiers carried it from the East to all parts of the Empire. *Neo-Platonism* was a religious philosophy which proposed to take the place of declining paganism. It reached its full development in the school founded by Ammonius Saccas (d. 243), which Origen attended. *Plotinus* (d. 270) was the real founder of the system and *Porphyry* gathered together the fifty-four treatises which explain his doctrine, as the 'Enneads'. The system was based on a *new theodicy*. Three moments, a kind of Trinity, must be distinguished in God – Being in itself; Intellect; Soul (which is the world-soul). Individual souls are emanations from this last. The human (spiritual) soul frees itself from matter (of the body) and returns to the world-soul, then to the Intellect and finally to Being itself. The return to God is by asceticism, illumination, and lastly ecstasy. Educated men found this attractive. In the system there were radical differences from Christianity – the Trinity and the moral and mystical doctrine which leads to union with God. In their system the union is not by grace, but by intellectual abstraction; no importance is attached to prayer; virtue has no moral character, and is only the soul's effort to free itself from matter.

Manichaeism was originally a pagan sect, then borrowed

from Christianity and became a heresy. Manes (b. 215) preached in Asia Minor as a prophet of a new revelation. He was put to death in 276. The essence of his teaching is *dualism*. There are two eternal kingdoms – Light (God's) and Darkness (Satan's). Man is made a prisoner by Satan and becomes the subject of struggle between God and his angel. The freeing of man is accomplished by severe asceticism. The society comprises Elect (monks) and Auditors (faithful). It spread rapidly in East and West, and lasted until the Middle Ages.

Christian Doctrinal Environment. There was a certain amount of opposition (in Rome, Carthage, and Alexandria) between those who were content with the traditional forms of popular faith, and those who wanted a scholarly theology which sought to make the formulas richer by philosophical speculation. The mystery of the *Trinity* was one that the theologians sought to expound while defending it. The monotheism of the Jews (stressed, too, by the first Christians) seemed difficult to reconcile with the divinity of Jesus Christ and the Holy Ghost. Gnostic dualism made it especially necessary to insist on the unity of God. The *Alexandrians* stressed philosophical tendencies. They preferred to consider the Divine Persons in their relations with creatures, not proceeding to consider God in Himself. They were concerned with the return of the soul to God, through Christ, the Way, and the Holy Ghost, his Messenger. This implies a kind of subordinationism 'but it is entirely exterior to the interior life of God'. There is no subordinationism in Clement, and less than appears in Origen, who is in no sense a forerunner of Arius. *Penance* and *baptism* of *heretics* gave rise to disciplinary controversies (vid. Hippolytus, Tertullian, Novatian, St. Cyprian).

Trinitarian Errors. *Modalism* denied the holding Trinity, maintaining one and the same Person is God, called Father, Son, and Holy Ghost under different *modes* or points of view. It was first called *Monarchianism*, and later *Patripassianism* (Father considered identical with the Son, and having suffered). *Praxeas*, who taught it, came from Asia to Rome to denounce Montanism and later went to Carthage where he was exposed by Tertullian. *Noetus* was refuted by Hippolytus. *Sabellius* was the author of Sabellianism (in the reign of Pope Zephyrinus or Callistus). The older system dealt with the Father and Son only. *Unitarianism* (Modalism proper) considered the Holy Ghost, too, and rejected Patripassianism. It taught that God is unity (the Father-Son), called the Word as Creator, Father as Law-giver, Son as Redeemer, Holy Ghost as Sanctifier. There is only one Person. God ceases to be Father in order to become the Son (who alone suffered), but the modes are equal, and there is no subordinationism.

Adoptianism denied the unity of the divine Persons and began by denying the Son's divinity. Christ is not God, but is *adopted* by God. Theodotus (a rich leather-seller of Byzantium), Theodotus (the Banker), and Artemas were the chief names. **Paul of Samosata** was a bishop and tax-gatherer at Antioch (c. 260) who denied Christ's divinity. He was attacked at the Council of Antioch (264) and resorted to ambiguity, and at a later Council (268) was deposed. Supported by Queen Zenobia, he refused to give up the Church property but it was handed over to the Church in 272 by the Emperor Aurelian (future persecutor). He taught a modalist form of Adoptianism, and did away with the personality of the Son and Holy Ghost. Christ, he held, was a man united to wisdom residing in Him by the virtue of God. This was the forerunner of Nestorianism. Attempts to rehabilitate him (F. Loofs) as a representative of the oldest Christian tradition which based its philosophy on Stoicism, was unitarian in theology, and favoured dualism in its Christology, have not been successful.

    Orientals. In the stress of controversy, history, exegesis and philosophy had helped in the defence of the faith, and the need for a fully scientific treatment of revealed truth, with all these valuable auxiliaries used to the full, was felt. The impulse to write had so far come from outside, from paganism or from heresy. Henceforth there was to be, within the Church herself, a comparatively peaceful growth of literary activity. This new development originated in the East, where were to be found all the great speculative thinkers, and its beginnings, though unknown, are associated with the *catechetical school of Alexandria* which appears already flourishing in A.D. 180. Pantaenus took over what was probably a school of catechumens, and even then, in 180, it was a famous Christian academy where all Greek science was studied and used to defend Christianity. Under Clement and Origen it reached its greatest fame, a fame which began to decrease in the fourth century. Scientific study was taken up in Jerusalem by Alexander, its bishop, former disciple of Pantaenus and Origen. He founded a theological library there. About 233 when Origen went to Palestine he

58

opened a school at Caesarea which became as renowned for science as Alexandria. Pamphilus after 250 laboured actively at Caesarea and is credited with having founded the famous library that was so serviceable to Eusebius and Jerome, but the credit belongs to Origen. Alexandria spread its influence as far as Asia Minor. Gregory Thaumaturgus was a disciple of Origen (from Caesarea), and Methodius consistently opposed Origen's theology throughout his life.

THE ALEXANDRINES

CLEMENT OF ALEXANDRIA

Clement of Alexandria was born probably at Athens, of heathen parents, about A.D. 150. After extensive travels he came to Alexandria. There (180) he became a disciple of Pantaenus, his collaborator, then a priest and finally on his master's death he became leader of the catechetical school (200). The school closed during Septimius Severus's persecution (202) and Clement went to Alexander, bishop of Cappadocia, where he died (215 or 216). As a writer he begins a new phase in Church teaching. He added to his teacher's oral methods the written page and aimed at catering thus for a wider circle, and supplying it with a scientific exposition and establishment of Christianity, with a good basis in philosophy and contemporary thought. 'To the cause of Christianity, which he espoused with a generous zeal, he brought a highly gifted nature and an encyclopaedic knowledge'. He knew the Greek classics, Plato especially, and the early ecclesiastical writings. His diction is pure, style facile and smooth, but there is a looseness and irregularity in composition. He was the first to expound, with a moral and paedagogical purpose, the relations of philosophy and theology and it was due in great measure to him that Alexandria became a first-class centre of influence in the East eclipsing the Churches of Asia and Syria. 'If from that period Rome was the heart of the Catholic world, Alexandria was already the brain' (Prat). Clement was a pioneer in theology, and any slips he made are thus accounted for.

The Catechetical School of Alexandria, which seems to have been in existence from beginning of the Alexandrian Church, developed into a school of scientific theology (3rd century), the bishop naming the head of it. It was official and even in Origen's time was only in initial stages of organisation. All the different philosophies had a meeting-ground in Alexandria and reaction against Gnosticism in particular directed the energies of the School. The masters of the school, especially Clement and Origen, created a powerful intellectual movement which may be called the School of Alexandria.

Writings. (A) *Protrepticus: Paedagogus: Stromata* – these are three parts of one whole – a graduated introduction to Christianity. Pt. I *(Protrepticus)* is like the earlier apologies – 'Exhortation to the Heathen' and exposes the folly of pagan beliefs, contrasts the purity and nobility of the teaching of the prophets and of Christ. Result is taken to be conversion, and Pt. II *(Tutor)* proceeds to educate one as a Christian. In three books, it is a series of instructions in the detailed duties of Christian life – food, drink, feasts, amusements, etc. The first book discusses the educational purpose of the Logos and methods of education (love and mildness, with punitive justice). Pt. III, the *Stromata* ('Miscellanies' or 'Tapestries of scientific commentaries according to the true philosophy') aims at presenting a scientific account of the revealed truths of Christianity, but the contents are disappointing, as there is constant returning to Pts. I and II. In Book I he deals with philosophy, its importance and utility in defending Christianity; in II with the superiority of revelation; in III and IV he refers to two criteria that differentiate Christian and heretical Gnosis: (a) the striving for moral perfection visible in virginal and marital chastity; (b) love of God shown in martyrdom. Part V returns to the relations of true Gnosis and faith; VI and VII portray the true Gnostic (the personification of all Christian perfection).

(B) *Sketches*, or Outlines – *Hypotyposes* – is a series of notes in eight books on passages of the Old and New Testament; exegesis was allegorical, interspersed with digressions into dogma and history.

(C) *Quis dives Salvetur?* – a delightful homily on Mark X, 17-31, greatly appreciated in antiquity. He shows that wealth is not evil, but that attachment to it must be mortified. Many lost works, of which fragments in quotation remain.

His *doctrine* is sometimes slightly at variance with tradition, because of his aims (in philosophy) and his being a pioneer in the field.

I. *Moral and mystical teaching* is most important in him. Christians are divided into simple Christians and Gnostics – the difference being of degree (cf. 1 Cor. 2:6). Three elements enter into the nature of perfection (a) *Apatheia* in consequence of divine union, holy indifference – passions mastered, yet not torpor but labour of the soul is implied and resistance to temptation and mortification of the senses are demanded. (b) *Charity* is the summit of the Gnostic ascension, brings God with it, is the principle of union with God. (c) *Gnosis,* perfect knowledge is the leading element, elevated, religious knowledge that transforms religious life and makes one God's friend and familiar. The orthodox Alexandrian gnosis is distinguished from simple faith which it makes more perfect; from theological speculation which of itself does not imply the mystical light; and from contemplation proper which is infused and need imply no discursive activity. It is perfect meditative contemplation. Though there were disadvantages in this system (charity e.g., not 'gnosis', is 'the greatest of these'), it made Alexandria the intellectual focus of the East, was an off-set to the heretical gnosis, and kept many cultured men, whom Neo-Plotinism would have tempted, in the Church.

II. *Theology*. He undertook to combine with ecclesiastical tradition elements that are foreign to it. He borrowed from Greek philosophy, especially Plato, and held that as the Jews were led to Christianity through the Old Testament the Gentiles should come through philosophy. Only by philosophy can faith advance to gnosis. Faith is a concise knowledge of what is necessary and science a demonstration of what has been accepted. Faith is always the foundation of the spiritual edifice. Photius accused Clement of admitting two Logoi, erring in the Trinity, but possibly was wrong in accusing him. His doctrine on creation is generally exact. In his Christology he allowed a very attenuated form of Docetism to intrude.

ORIGEN

Origen (185-254-5), born in Egypt, in Alexandria, of Christian parents, received from his early education from Leonidas, his father (martyred, 202), frequented Clement's school, and so impressed his contemporaries by his brilliance that at the age of eighteen, in 203 (or 205), he was chosen to succeed Clement as president of the Alexandrian School. His teaching-life falls into two periods, A.D. 203-231, and 231-254, for the former of which he was in Alexandria, for the latter in Caesarea in Palestine. Into less than seventy years he crowded an amount of writing, teaching and instructing that passes comprehension, even when his staff of clerks (short-hand) and assistants is taken into account. He travelled to Rome and Caesarea. In 215 in the latter he preached before the bishop, and incurred the displeasure of his own bishop, Demetrius, for preaching as a layman. In 230 he went again to Caesarea on a mission for his bishop and was there ordained priest by Alexander, bishop of Jerusalem, and Theoctistus, bishop of Caesarea. Demetrius was very angry, removed him from headship of the school, degraded him from the priesthood, and Origen departed from Alexandria and made Caesarea the seat of a new school, the fame of which spread throughout the East. He journeyed from there to Africa and Arabia, was imprisoned and tortured during the Decian persecution (251), and died at Tyre shortly after being released. The chief sources of our information for his life are Eusebius, Pamphilus, Gregory Thaumaturgus, Jerome, Photius.

Works. He was the most extensive writer of all the early Fathers, about 2,000 titles being listed by Eusebius, about 800 by St. Jerome. We possess only a small remnant of his work, and only half of what remains is in Greek, the remainder in Latin versions. Jerome and Rufinus translated him, while Basil and Gregory of Nazianzus compiled an anthology *(Philokalia Origenis)*. Whole classes of his writings perished as a result of Justianian's edict (543), the adverse judgment of the Fifth General Council (553), and the attitude of the so-called Gelasian Decretal 'de libris recipiendis et non recipiendis', (books to be admitted or otherwise). Origen left works on biblical text-criticism, exegesis; commentaries on the greater part of the Scriptures; works on apologetic, polemical, dogmatic, ascetical questions; he outlined the entire field of theology. 'He was the first to construct a philosophico-theological system at once uniform and comprehensive. All the theological movements and schools belonging to the patristic period of the Greek Church are grouped about Origen as about a common centre of union or divergency'. (Bardenhewer). The chief classes of his work are:

I. **Biblical Work.** The *Hexapla* a 'gigantic enterprise', now lost. He copied in parallel columns (1) the Hebrew text of the Old Testament in Hebrew letters; (2) the Hebrew text in Greek letters; and in four succeeding columns the Greek versions of (a) Aquila, (b) Symmachus, (c) the Septuagint, and (d) Theodotion. a, b, d, were private versions; c semi-official. The title means the 'six-fold writing'. Begun at Alexandria, it was finished probably at Tyre. Only fragments remain of the Greek, but the greater part of it has reached us in a Syriac version made in 616 or 617 by Paul, bishop of Tella.

II. **Biblico-Exegetical Writings** are divided into (a) *Scholia*. (b) *Homilies*, and (c) *Commentaries*, i.e. (a) brief notes on

63

difficult points of Sacred Scripture; (b) popular expositions, (c) exhaustive and learned notes. Neglecting almost entirely the historical sense, he dwells in these on the mystical sense, and employs the allegorical mode of interpretation in vogue in Alexandria. He felt there were many hard and repulsive things in the Scriptures taken literally and historically, and distinguished between a carnal and spiritual sense. His knowledge of Hebrew was modest, and the main ideal of the *Hexapla* is apologetic usefulness rather than textual criticism. He felt that the Septuagint was divinely inspired.

III. **Apologetic Works.** The chief one is *Contra Celsum*, (see p. 38). Celsus's *Alethes Logos* was a violent attack on Christianity and a defence of the State religion. Origen refutes him point by point in this, the most perfect apologetic work of the early Church. Nowhere has he shown greater ability or learning. It was in eight books, and has been preserved in a thirteenth century Vatican codex, and portion of it (one-seventh) in the *Philokalia*. Other, anti-heretical, works have been lost.

IV. **Dogmatic Writings.** The originals have been lost. The most important was *De Principiis*, (Peri Archon). In four books, it treats of the fundamental principles of the Christian religion. We have fragments in the *Philokalia* and all of it in a paraphrase by Rufinus. (1) God and the world of spirits; (2) the world and man, redemption of man, his end; (3) human freedom and final triumph of the good; (4) Scriptural interpretation. Composed at Alexandria (230) it is the earliest attempt at a scientific exposition of Christianity. In several points it departed from ecclesiastical tradition, and aroused opposition as well as admiration.

Second work was *Miscellanies* – fragments remain.

V. **Ascetic Works** and **Homilies.** 1 (a) On Prayer; (b) On the Lord's Prayer. 2 Exhortation to Martyrdom, and others.

VI. **Letters** – several volumes, but only two letters remain, one to Julius Africanus, and one to St. Gregory Thaumaturgus.

Characteristics. To contrast false Gnosis with true Christian knowledge, and to win educated minds to the latter, Origen undertook to combine Hellenic philosophy with the faith. His doctrinal system was really tainted with Neoplatonism and Gnosticism, and he unconsciously fell into error while seeking to defend truth. He constructed the first summa of Theology. His renown, during his life, world-wide; his writings were read and used by different parties in the Trinitarian controversy. He influenced the leading men in the East and West down to the end of the fourth century. His weakness lay in reliance on philosophy rather than on the Gospel. 'Three great doctrines in Origen's system – the eternal creation of the world, the pre-existence of the soul, the final restoration of all intelligent creatures to God's friendship – are echoes of Platonic and Neo-Platonic philosophy in points fundamentally unchristian'. The supplanting of Platonic Idealism by Aristotelian Realism 'gave an impetus to an anti-Origenist movement which had arisen within a century of Origen's death, and which was based partly on Origen's errors, partly on vague statements in his works, and partly on personal dispute, with which Origen had only accidental connection'. After he had nourished the greatest of the Eastern doctors, his name became a by-word throughout the Byzantine Middle Ages. In the West, however, fate was more kind to him. His writings were read, Bede and Bernard respected him, and he continued to excite admiration'. In 543 the Synod of Constantinople condemned fifteen propositions from his works; in 553 the Fifth General Council ranked him with 'heretics'. 'Directly and indirectly, comprehended and misinterpreted, he is the founder of theology, and all things considered, the most influential of the Greek Fathers. We shall meet greater literary artists in our survey of the Greek Fathers, and men with a greater personal following in the West. We shall not meet a greater individual force'. (Campbell).

DIONYSIUS OF ALEXANDRIA

Dionysius of Alexandria was born at the end of the second century, a heathen, was converted, and attended the School of Alexandria when Origen was head. He succeeded Heraclas as head of the school (231-232), and seems to have retained office after he had succeeded Heraclas (247-248) as bishop of Alexandria. His episcopate was very troubled, and he escaped the Decian persecution by flight (250-251). In the Valerian persecution he was banished to Kephro (257) and on his return in 262 found civil war, famine, and pestilence in his see. He died in 264 (during the Synod of Antioch, which he was too ill to attend). He had a great reputation – called by Eusebius 'the great', by Athanasius 'Doctor of the Church', for his

65

eminence as a public figure. His writings are occasional, his diction clear and lively, his exposition often obscure. We have a few fragments in Eusebius.

Works. I. Books on Nature *(Peri Physeos)*, against Epicureanism, in 247. II. Book on Temptations. III. Two Books on the Promises, against Nepos, a bishop, who defended the historical interpretation of Scripture (especially the Apocalypse and the Millenium). His orthodoxy became suspect concerning the Trinity – he was supposed to have fallen into Sabellianism through overstatement of the distinction between the Father and the Son. His defence, to Pope Dionysius (259-268) in a letter, and in four books, seems to have satisfied the Pope. We have fragments in Athanasius and Basil.

Letters urging Novatian to submit to Pope Cornelius are of great interest, also a letter to Fabius of Antioch.

Later Headmasters of Alexandrian School. Theognostus; Pierius; Peter of Alexandria.

The so-called **Apostolic Church Order** purports to emanate from the twelve Apostles. The Way of Life is simply a modified version of the Two Ways in the *Didache*. It was composed probably in Egypt towards the end of the third century. It is a valuable source of ecclesiastical law. Bickell published the Greek original in 1843. There are Latin, Syriac, Arabic, Ethiopic and Coptic versions. See *Church Orders*.

SYRO – PALESTINIANS

JULIUS AFRICANUS

Julius Africanus, a Libyan, seems to have been an officer in the army of Septimius Severus (195). About 211 he visited Alexandria, and attended Heraclas's lectures. He died after A.D. 240.

Two Works. 1. *Chronographia* – a universal chronicle in five books (221) was an attempt to harmonise Jewish and Christian history with the history of the Gentile world. He took certain dates from the Bible, and tried to order the chief events in world history. This first of Christian world-chronicles has rendered substantial service to Eusebius.

2. *Embroidered Girdles (Kestoi)* (14, or 24 books) is dedicated to Alexander Severus, and is an extensive encyclopaedia of natural sciences, medicine, magic, agriculture, naval and military warfare. Fragments remain. A *letter* of Africanus to

Origen (about Susanna in Daniel) has been preserved. Eusebius thought highly of it.

PAUL OF SAMOSATA. MALCHION OF ANTIOCH. LUCIAN OF SAMOSATA

Paul of Samosata was bishop of Antioch from 260. He taught that Christ was only man. Three synods were held in Antioch (264-269) as a result, and Malchion, a priest and a teacher of rhetoric, exposed his heresy and Paul was deposed and excommunicated. We have shorthand notes of the discussion between them. Malchion is supposed to be the author of the encyclical letter of the synod making the affair known to the Catholic world.

Lucian of Samosata, Presbyter of Antioch and founder of the Antiochene exegetical school, shared Paul's views, was probably excommunicated with him, and recanted. He was martyred at Nicomedia (7 Jan. 312). He made a critical revision of the Septuagint and of the Gospels.

PAMPHILUS OF CAESAREA. DIALOGUS DE RECTA IN DEUM FIDE. DIDASCALLA APOSTOLORUM.

Pamphilus of Caesarea was born at Berytus in Phoenicia, studied theology at Alexandria and lived then at Caesarea, where he was ordained priest. He opened a theological school there and in 309 suffered martyrdom under Maximinus. He is important for his building up of the library of Caesarea. In prison he wrote an *apologia* for Origen (5 books), refuting charges of heterodoxy against him.

Dialogus de Recta in Deum Fide is the work of an unknown author, in five books, against the Gnostics, 300-310. It is under Origen's name, the reason being probably because the name Adamantius (the man of steel, Origen) is in the title.

The **Didascalia Apostolorum** is a work on Christian morality, Church-constitution, and Christian discipline, resembling the *Didache*. A Syriac version exists. It treats, after a general exhortation to Christians, of the qualifications for the office of bishops, their duties and rights, law-suits, liturgical assemblies, care of the poor, fasting, heresy. It is pseudo-Apostolic.

The *Didascalia* is Syriac and was written in Syria in the first

67

half or first decades (Altaner, Quasten) of the third century. It is also known as the 'Catholic Teaching of the Twelve Apostles and Holy Disciples of Our Saviour', and Epiphanius calls it *Diataxeis ton apostolon*. The author was a bishop, probably a Jew, and had evidently been a doctor; he shows no special theological acumen. It was directed to a community of Christians in northern Syria, converts from paganism. It shows itself severe towards Jews who regard the Jewish law as obligatory on Christians. In contrast to the contemporary western writers (Tertullian, Hippolytus, Cyprian) its tone is gentle, mild towards sinners, conceding readmission to the Church merely with imposition of hands and a fast of a few days. It borrows from the *Didache*, Gospel of Peter, Acts of Paul, Ignatius, Hermas and Irenaeus. The Greek text is lost but we have a Syriac translation. The work is the chief source of the first six books of the *Apostolic Constitutions*. Its lost Greek original is the basis of the Arabic and the Ethiopic Didascalia. (See *Apostolic Tradition* and *Church Orders* p. 61)

WRITERS OF ASIA MINOR

ST. GREGORY THAUMATURGUS

St. Gregory, the Wonder-Worker, in his panegyric on Origen gives information about his own life. He was born about 213 of a noble heathen family at Neo-Caesarea in Pontus, studied law, and he and his brother Athenodorus were about to study law at Berytus when circumstances brought them to Caesarea in Palestine. There, in 233, they fell under Origen's spell, turned to philosophy and theology and were converted by Origen. They remained for five years and on their depature in 238 Gregory delivered a public panegyric on Origen. Both of them were made bishops in Pontus, Gregory becoming first bishop of his native Neo-Caesarea then largely pagan. His *Life* by St. Gregory of Nyssa relates a long series of miraculous happenings which earned for him the title 'Wonder-Worker'. Whatever their authenticity, the growth of the legends testifies to St. Gregory's superior personality and successful labours. He died about 270, having converted the population of Neo-Caesarea.

Works. He wrote little, and only as the occasion demanded it. (1) *Panegyric on Origen* in 238. (2) *Creed of Gregory*, 260-270 – a brief exposition of the doctrine of the Trinity. (3) The *Canonical Epistle*, written to solve the doubts of a bishop about the treatment of Christians who had violated discipline and morality during the raids of the Goths. It is important in the history of ecclesiastical discipline. It was mild.

ST. METHODIUS OF OLYMPUS

St. Methodius of Olympus. Little is known of him, and Eusebius does not mention him. He was bishop of Olympus in Lycia and was martyred in 311 under Maximinus Daza. His chief claim to fame is based on his literary work. He was a stylist, diffuse, pleasant, elegant. He conducted a determined and successful fight against Origenism. We have only one work in Greek – others are preserved in Old Slavonic.

Works. (1) *The Banquet on Virginity (Symposion, Peri hAgeneias)* – praise of virginity, in the form of a banquet. It is an imitation of Plato's 'Banquet'. (2) *On the Freedom of the Will* (we have almost all the Greek version). It attacks Gnostic dualism and determinism, denies the eternity of matter as a principle of evil. Evil is said to result from freewill. (3) *On the Resurrection* – a dialogue.

THE WESTERN WRITERS

The western literature is in Latin, is Roman in spirit, sober, practical, with less idealism and less tendency to speculation than the Greek writings. Its purpose is generally the necessary and the useful. There is great variety and versatility in writings and authors. The apologetic element is predominant – Tertullian and Hippolytus (Greek). Hippolytus and Victorinus of Pettau represent exegesis. Commodian is the first of the Christian-Latin poets. The writers are few, and mainly from Africa. One great task confronting them was terminology. This is one of their great triumphs, the invention, the fashioning of technical language, and the chief glory for it goes to Tertullian, who exercised a tremendous influence on Western theology.

AFRICAN WRITERS

TERTULLIAN

Tertullian. Quintus Septimius Florens Tertullianus was born in Carthage in 160, son of a centurion in the service of the proconsul of Africa. He received a very thorough education, studied law and became an advocate. About 193 he became a Christian, and was ordained priest and began a long literary career in defence of Christianity. About 202 or 205 he became a Montanist and attacked Catholicism violently. He founded the Tertullianists, and lived to a very advanced age (d. after A.D. 220). He is the most prolific of all the Latin writers, most original and personal. In no one else is Buffon's phrase, 'the style is the man', more justified (Ebert) – he always spoke from the heart. His writings are (1) apologetic; (2) dogmatico-polemic; (3) practico-ascetical. The personal note is always present, whether he writes carried away with a holy zeal that is harshly rigorous, or as a Montanist raging against the alleged laxity of the Catholic Church. A born controversialist, powerful adversary, eloquent and fiery, a man of biting satire and compact logic, he often overshoots the mark, writes without moderation, sweeps away opposition rather than convinces. His expression is bold, concise, rugged, involved; he does not bother with beauty of form – he is 'daringly creative and suddenly enriches the Latin tongue'. With St. Augustine he is the greatest Western theologian. Western theology is in his debt for many technical terms. Indeed, in a sense, he created the clear language of Western theology.

Works. (A) Apologetic Writings. I. *Apologeticum* (or *Apologeticus liber*) is one of his finest works (c. 197). Addressed to Roman provincial governors, it falls into two parts: (1) treatment of charges of secret crimes amongst Christians; (2) public crimes. The second class were contempt of State religion, and high treason. He refutes these, and concludes with the assertion of the absolute superiority of Christianity over all, as a revealed religion. The work of a trained Roman lawyer, its legal refutation is very important. The relation between this and M. Felix *(Octavius)* is not clear. II. *Ad Nationes*, 2 books (c. 197) ridicules heathen worship (draws on Varro's *Rerum Divinarium Libri XVI*) and shows that the accusations made against Christianity are true of paganism. III. *Ad Scapulam*, (c. 212), a brief letter to the proconsul in Africa, a persecutor. Tertullian reminds him of the fate that befell other persecutors. IV. *Adversus Judaeos* – a discussion to prove that the Israelites rejected God's grace.

(B) Dogmatico-Polemical Works. I. *De Praescriptione Hereticorum*, Tertullian's 'imperishable work', is the defence of Christianity and refutation of heresy as such. Praescriptio – form of procedure based on length of possession – excludes the accuser at the opening of the process. He treats of the origin and nature of heresy, and elaborates Irenaeus's position, i.e. that only in apostolic writers and churches can truth be found. Heresy is a usurper, a late-comer; heretics have no right to use Sacred Scripture which has been given to the Church. By prescription Catholics are in possession of the truth. In conclusion he points out the evil effects of heresy in the life of the heretic. It is 'a classic defence of the Catholic principle of authority and tradition – a development of the theory of St. Irenaeus, set forth with the skill of a jurist'. II. *Adversus Marcionem*, (5 books) was revised twice, and edited in 207. Books 1 and 2 refute Marcion's dualism; Book 3 proves the historical Christ is the Messias foretold in the Old Testament. Books 4 and 5 are a criticism of Marcion's Gospel and Epistles. III. *Adversus Hermogenem*, (a painter) also attacks dualism.

71

IV. *Adversus Valentinianos* (a Montanist work). V. *De Baptismo*, (Catholic work) defends the traditional teaching against the 'poisonous viper' Quintilla, and declares heretical baptism invalid. VI. *De Carne Christi* – polemical work against the Gnostic Docetism of Marcion etc. – Christ was really man, with a human body. VII. The *Scorpiace*, or antidote against the bites of scorpions, is against the Gnostics, and shows the meritorious nature of martyrdom. VIII. *De Resurrectione Carnis* – reality of it, against the Gnostics. IX. *Adversus Praxeam* – his last anti-heretical writing, long after his exit from the Church, defends the ecclesiastical teaching on the Trinity against Patripassian monarchianism. In many expressions and turns of thought he almost forestalls the Nicene Creed.

Practico-Ascetical Writings. (1) *De Patientia*. (2) *De Oratione* – on the Lord's Prayer, and prayer in general; (3) *De Poenitentia*, gives ecclesiastical practice of the time – public canonical penances for different sins. (4) *De Pudicitia*, (Montanist) goes back on the former attitude, fiercely attacks Pope Callistus for holding that adultery and fornication can be forgiven (see Penance Tract). (5) *Ad Martyres*, – a beautiful letter of exhortation, c. 197. (6) *Ad Uxorem* – on marriage and re-marriage (addressed to his wife, Esther). As a Montanist, he rejects second marriages utterly. In *De Monogamia* and before it, in *De Exhortatione Castitatis*, he declares second marriage sinful – 'species stupri', *a sort of adultery* (217). *De Spectaculis* answers, in the negative, the question: is it lawful for Christians to frequent the public games and theatres (spectacula)? The reason is that they are associated with idolatry, and arouse passion. 'He pours out against heathenism all the hatred of his soul in a flaming description of the greatest spectacle the world shall ever behold, the Second Coming of Our Lord'. *De Idolatria*, (Catholic) deals with the occasions and dangers of idolatry in life. *De Corona*, (211) – apropos of the refusal of a soldier to wear a crown – of the rites of idolatry. *De Cultu Feminarum*, (2 books) (Catholic) denounces female vanity in dress and ornament (known also as *De Habitu Muliebri*). *De Virginibus Velandis*, departed from his position in *De Oratione* and maintained virgins everywhere and always should be veiled. *De Fuga in Persecutione* (Montanist) absolutely forbids flight (212). *De Anima* was written as a Montanist, is the first Christian psychology and aims at giving true Christian idea of the soul, against Gnostics, (a) nature and faculties of the soul which has some degree of corporeity, and (b) origin of each soul. He adopts the crassest generationism or traducianism; (c) treats of death, sleep, world of dreams, place of the soul after death. *De Pallio*, (209) justifies his act of discarding the toga and adopting the pallium.

ST. CYPRIAN ✓

St. Cyprian, Bishop of Carthage, Martyr. 'One of the most attractive figures in early ecclesiastical literature is the noble bishop of Carthage, Thascius Caecilius Cyprianus'. The *Vita Caecili Cypriani*, the first biography of him, ascribed to Pontius, a deacon, and St. Cyprian's works and the *Acta* of his martyrdom are the chief sources of our information. St. Jerome *(De Vir. Ill.)* and others give much biographical detail also. Born about 200 in Africa of wealthy pagan parents, he was educated at the best centres of learning, and became a rhetorician. He attained great eminence in the most outstanding career in Africa, 'the nurse of pleaders', as a teacher of rhetoric at Carthage, the capital of Africa and its chief seat of learning and eloquence. About 246 he was converted by a priest, Caecilius or Caecilianus (whose name he took), and was admitted to the clergy. At the end of 248, or more probably the beginning of 249, he was elected bishop of Carthage, becoming thereby metropolitan of Africa.

His episcopate of ten years was a most momentous one in the history of the Church, and he guided with great success the Church of Africa through the trials of the Decian persecution, a fearful plague (like the Black Death) which swept through and devastated the Roman Empire, and the initial stages of the Valerian persecution; and he was the central figure in great disciplinary disputes and domestic perils which threatened the Church much more seriously than the persecutions. The African Church had little opportunity, and little taste, for speculation. Its life was a life of action, and its literature a reflection of that life. From the Christian literature of the time St. Cyprian's is the greatest personality that comes down to posterity. He was the embodiment of the finest ideals of that life and literature. His writings have a peculiarly personal quality. The Numidian bishops, convicts in the mines during the Valerian persecution, wrote to him: 'In all the excellences which thou hast inscribed in thy many books thou hast unknowingly portrayed thyself to us'. He brought to his high office an ardent, living faith, a burning charity, a firmness of character which never degenerated into harshness, exceptional administrative ability; a knowledge of men and affairs, prudence, talents of mind, all the personal graces and charms that made him one of the outstanding figures in the highest profession in the land.

During the Decian persecution (250-251) he fled from Carthage (on divine guidance, he explained, and for the sake of the Church), and many renounced the faith. The apostates were *sacrificati*, *thurificati*, or *libellatici*, Christians who had offered sacrifice or incense to the gods or obtained a certificate (libellus) that they had done so. The question of restoring these *lapsi* to the Church, and the penance to be done by them, occasioned a schism in Rome and Carthage. The lax party in Carthage were led by a deacon, Felicissimus, and elected a bishop (Fortunatus) in Carthage for themselves. Novatus, a laxist, fled from Carthage to Rome, and for policy allied himself with Novatian, the Puritan, who had found the Pope, St. Cornelius, too lenient on the reconciliation question, and who had himself, Novatian, elected bishop, and anti-pope. (This party sent a rigorist bishop, Maximus, to Carthage to oppose Cyprian). The laxist party found little support and soon disappeared. The Novatian party, the rigorists, secured imperial favour occasionally, were better organised, and lasted on until the sixth century, 'a stern Puritan relic of the Decian persecution'. Another result of the Decian persecution was the Baptism controversy, on the validity of baptism conferred by heretics. Cyprian held, with Tertullian, that such baptism was invalid, and he baptized anew all who returned to the Church if they had received baptism in heresy. Several Councils held in Carthage between 255 and 256 upheld this decision. Pope Stephen I (Saint) rejected this view and declared 'Si qui ergo a quacunque haeresi venient ad vos, nihil innovetur nisi quod traditum est, ut manus illis imponatur in paenitentian', (Cyprian, Ep. 74,1). 'If people therefore come to you from any heresy whatever, let nothing be innovated which has not been handed down; namely, that hands be imposed upon them for their repentance'. This controversy threatened to disrupt the unity of the whole Western Church. (The African Church quietly dropped their practice in later times.) The persecution of Valerian and the death of the Pope, prevented a formal conflict, and amicable relations were restored between his

74

successor and St. Cyprian. St. Cyprian was martyred, beheaded in the Valerian persecution, 14 September 258, in the gardens of the proconsular Vila Sexti, near Carthage. The *Acta Proconsularia,* – official record of his execution – is extant. St. Cyprian is celebrated in the highest terms of praise by all antiquity as a perfect model of a Catholic bishop and pastor and administrator. His works were accorded an honour only short of that given to the canonical books. (There are almost as many MSS. of his works as of the Scriptures, going back to the sixth century).

Writings. His writings are of two main groups: (1) *Letters,* (2) *Treatises.* He does not indulge in speculations, but concerns himself with the needs of the hour, with practical aims and interests, appeals to Christian sentiments, to Scripture. He is always moderate and mild. In many of his works he relies on and borrows openly from Tertullian whom, with the Scriptures, he read daily. *Da magistrum,* he said, asking for Tertullian, (Jerome, *De Vir. Ill.,* 53). In dealing with St. Cyprian as a theologian it is necessary to remember that he had only twelve years of life as a Christian; that beyond the Scriptures he had little or nothing to guide him except Tertullian, who was often exaggerated in his claims and views; and that the labours and trials of his episcopate left him little time for theological speculation. He was a man of action primarily. His own personality is stamped on all his works – he was a refined scholar and conducted into 'smooth channels the turbid waters of his master's eloquence'. His diction is free, clear, pleasing and classical; his language always enlivened and exalted by his warm generous feelings. 'Quite frequently the page is coloured by images and allegories chosen with taste and finished with skilful attention to the smallest detail; not a few of them became more or less the commonplaces of later ecclesiastical literature'. In his letters we see Church life as it was actually lived – the contact between the different sees, the burning interest which all questions of discipline had for laity and clergy alike, the excesses of vice of which Africa was capable, and the heights of heroism to which it could rise. In them, we can see the consummate skill and diplomacy of Cyprian at work, his indefatigable energy, the gradual growth of confidence in, and submission to, his administration by the whole African Church. His treatises have not the same charm nor have they the same interest. The best of them draw their excellence from the same source as the letters – from action, and the circumstances of the time, e.g. *De Lapsis* and *De Catholicae Ecclesiae Unitate*.

Letters. The collection contains eighty-one Letters, sixty-five from his own hand, sixteen sent to him or to Carthage clergy. Twenty-seven during the Decian persecution – twelve treat of the Novatian schism; eleven praise the confessors; twelve refer to the Roman Church. Letter s76-81 were written during the Valerian persecution (257-258). 'In letter 76 we have an admirable message of consolation from the exiled bishop to the martyrs in the mines. In letter 81 the shepherd of Carthage, while awaiting a martyr's death, sends to his flock a final salutation'.

Treatises. Thirteen are extant.

(a) *Quod idola dii non sint* (246), while still a catechumen.

(b) *Ad Donatum* – a highly coloured, poetical description of the new life entered on by baptismal regeneration (c. 246).

(c) *De habitu virginum* (resembles Tertullian's work) – against vanity in dress etc., a pastoral letter to women dedicated to God (c. 249).

(d) *De Lapsis* (251) composed on his return to Carthage after the Decian persecution on the fallen brethren, laments their fall and states conditions for return to the Church.

(e) *De Catholicae Ecclesiae Unitate* – 'an immortal work' – a forcible exposition and defence of the Church to which alone were made the promises of salvation, and not to the schisms of Rome and Carthage. Contrary to the old opinion, this was not composed in view of the Novatian schism, nor in 251, but later; nor was it read at the first council of Carthage. Chap. IV maintains very strongly the claims of Rome as supreme and around it has raged a literary war between Protestants and Catholics. The pro-Petrine text (the long one) is genuine and was first written. The shorter one, less enthusiastic about Rome, is Cyprian's also (Bevenot, S.J. – MSS. study of Chap. IV). This is Cyprian's most outstanding treatise. It attacks schism (that of Felicissimus probably) and urges the necessity of union with the one Catholic Church which is compared with Christ's seamless robe (c. 7). He sent it to Rome to combat the violence of the Novatianists. Christ founded His Church on one, on Peter; the unity of the foundation guarantees the unity of the edifice. Schism and heresy are from Satan. 'Habere non potest Deum patrem qui ecclesiam non habet matrem', 'He cannot have God for his

Father who does not have the Church for his Mother.'
(c. 6).
(f) *De Dominica Oratione* (251-2) – like Tertullian's.
(g) *Ad Demetrianum* – apologetic (c. 252) – address to a
magistrate proving that famine, war, pestilence are
attributed wrongly to Christian neglect of pagan gods, and
are sent really as punishment for the treatment of Christians.
(h) *De Mortalitate* – a magnificent discourse of consolation on
the occasion of the pestilence in 252, 'breathing in every
line a magnanimity of soul and a power of faith that are
most touching'.
(i) *De opere et eleemosynis* – an exhortation to charity.
(k) *De bono patientiae* – 256 – during the baptism controversy,
and an attempt to stem the rising tide of angry feeling.
(l) *De zelo et livore* – 256 – same origin.
(m) *Ad Fortunatum.* Collection of texts exhorting and en-
couraging one to suffer martyrdom (the Valerian persecution was raging), 257.
(n) *Ad Quirinum vel Testimoniorum Libri*: (248) – a collection
of biblical texts of great importance for our study of the
Bible.

(See 'The African Church and the Decian Persecution', *Ir.
Eccl. Record*, May/June/July 1942; and 'The Church in Africa
in the Third Century', ibid, October 1943, by P. J. Hamell.)

ARNOBIUS

Arnobius flourished in Proconsular Africa under Diocetian
(284-305) at Sicca and taught rhetoric with distinction. As a
result of a dream he was converted and approached the bishop
of Sicca for reception as a Christian. The bishop was doubtful
about his conversion, and Arnobius, to prove his sincerity,
composed a polemical work against heathenism during the
Diocletian persecution (303-305) – *Adversus Nationes* (7 books).
Books 1-2 are a defence of Christianity – vindication from
charges. Books 3-7 attack pagan superstition and mythology.
His learning was superficial, his style and talent noteworthy,
his knowledge of Christian doctrine slight. The second part of
the work is the better part.

77

Lactantius. Lucius Caelius Firmianus Lactantius was born about 250 in Africa, of heathen parents. He won fame in Africa as a rhetorician, and Diocletian summoned him to be a professor at Nicomedia. He tells the story of his journey in a poem (lost). Converted in 303, he resigned his position in the same year when the persecution broke out, and lived in utter destitution. About 317 Constantine invited him to teach Crispus, his son, at Trier. He may have been a pupil of Arnobius. We know nothing of the time or manner of his death. He was more successful in attacking paganism than defending Christianity. 'Utinam tam nostra afirmare potuisset quam facile aliena destruxit', 'I wish that he could have upheld our heritage with as much ease as he destroyed others'. (St. Jerome, Ep. 58, 10). Comprehensive and versatile, he has a natural, pleasing, restrained style, 'vir omnium suo tempore eloquentissimus, quasi quidam fluvius eloquentiae Tullianae', – 'The most eloquent men of his time, like a very fount of Tullian eloquence', (St. Jerome). Pico della Mirandola (1494) and other humanists called him the Christian Cicero. He was widely read and his works ran into several editions. 'The real strength of Lactantius lies in his formal grace and elegance of expression; like his heathen model he lacks solidity and depth'. Except for St. Jerome and perhaps St. Augustine, no Christian writer of antiquity was so deeply versed in Latin and Greek literature, but his knowledge of ecclesiastical literature was meagre. He tended towards chiliasm and dualism.

Works (a) *De Opificio Dei* (304 or 305?) treats of man, anatomically and physiologically, maintaining against the Epicureans that the human organism is a creation of God. Stoic ideas abound in it. (b) *Divinae Institutiones* (7 books) is his chief work, and was composed about 311, apologetic and theological in character. (It is commonly held that (a) – above – is an epitome of this and so subsequent to it). Pamphlets against Christianity after the Diocetian persecution occasioned it, and he aimed at refuting errors and expounding Christian teaching. Books I-II impugn polytheism and prove monotheism to be the only true religion. He outlines Christianity, concluding with a description of the after-life of the blessed in 3-7. (c) *De Ira Dei*, (310-312) against Stoics and Epicureans. (d) *De Mortibus Persecutorum* (313 or post 316) – an account of the terrible deaths of imperial persecutors – Nero, Domitian,

Valerian, Diocletian, Maximin, Severus – an argument is derived for the truth of Christianity. (e) *De Ave Phoenice* – a poem – relates the myth of the fabulous Eastern bird rising from its pyre to a new life every thousand years. It has a specific Christian colour, and is believed to be the work of Lactantius. There are, besides, lost works and spurious works, e.g. *De Resurrectione, De Passione Domini* (15th century).

ROMAN WRITERS

POPES

(1) *Soter* (c. 166-174) – Letter to the Corinthians (2) *Eleutherius* (174-189) (and St. Irenaeus). (3) *Victor I* (189-198) wrote about Montanism, Monarchianism, and the celebration of Easter. (4) *Zephyrinus* (198-217) defended the faith against different heresies. (5) *Callistus* (217-222) assailed by Hippolytus; excommunicated Sabellius. (6) *Pontianus* (230-235) wrote to Demetrius, bishop of Alexandria, c. 232 about a synod held in Rome. (7) *Cornelius* (251-253) – seven letters to Cyprian; we have two – three letters to Fabius, bishop of Antioch, on the Novatian schism. (8) *Lucius* (253-254) wrote about the Lapsed. Cf. Cyprian, Ep. 68,5. (9) *Stephen I* (254-257) – Letters to Syria, Arabia, Asia, Cyprian about the baptism controversy. (10) *Sixtus II* (257-258). (11) *Dionysius* (259-268) – Letters about Sabellianism and Subordinationism. (12) *Felix* (269-274) – known for his connection with the condemnation of Paul of Samosata. (13) *Miltiades* (311-314).

ST. HIPPOLYTUS OF ROME

St. Hippolytus (c. 170-235) was of noble birth (Greek or Latin by nationality). He wrote in Greek. A disciple of St. Irenaeus, he was ordained by Pope Victor, and became a celebrated writer. Very little was known of his life until the nineteenth century. The first important document discovered (1551) was a list of his works inscribed on a marble statue of Hippolytus in a sitting position, dating from third century, in the 'cemetery of Hippolytus' on the Via Tiburtina, erected by his admirers. A second important discovery was the *Philosophumena*, at Mt. Athos, in 1842. This was published in 1851 under Origen's name, subsequently ascribed to Tertullian, Caius of Rome, and Novatian. Dollinger vindicated the authorship of Hippolytus. He may have been born 170-175. Origen, in Rome, heard a sermon preached by him in 212. He died a martyr under Maximinus the Thracian about 235. Scriptural work, defence of the faith, personal controversies – these represent the three phases of his life. The favour and promotion given to Callistus in Rome (Callistus was of humble origin), by Pope Zephyrinus, roused envy and anger in Hippolytus. Callistus became Pope in 217. Hippolytus, head of the opposition, became anti-pope because of his previous animosity and theological and disciplinary differences. Hippolytus, in attacking Sabellianism, unconsciously defended a form of Subordinationism; Callistus under Zephyrinus defended monarchy in such fashion that Hippolytus accused him of Sabellianism and was accused by him of 'Ditheismus', holding two Gods. He attacked Callistus, as Pope, for laxity in forgiving murder, adultery, fornication. Cf. Edict of Callistus. Callistus mitigated the severity of the penitential discipline somewhat, and the rigorists (Hippolytus) said this would lead to spread of crime. Tertullian violently assailed this Edict of Callistus in *De Pudicitia*, (Montanist). 'Audio etiam edictum esse propositum, et quidem peremptorium, Pontifex scilicet maximus... episcopus episcoporum, edicit. Ego et moechiae et fornicationis delicta poenitentia functis dimitto. O edictum cui adscribi non poterit bonum factum', 'I hear too that an edict has been published – and one of the fullest authority at that – i.e. the High Priest... bishop of bishops has decreed: I remit the sins of adultery and fornication to those who have done penance. What an edict! – no good will be ascribed to it'. (probably Tertullian's attack was on Agrippinus of Carthage). From 217-235 the schism continued, Hippolytus having a considerable following. In 235 he was banished with the Pope, Pontianus, to Sardinia, became reconciled with many of his followers and died a martyr. He was buried with Pontianus in Rome, and his supporters erected a statue to him.

Eusebius and Jerome knew little about him. Damasus (c. 366) and Prudentius (c. 404, poet), who wrote about him, knew little either. Hippolytus was a man of profound learning and thorough education, and ranks as one of the great figures of the third century in theology. Sincerely orthodox at heart, he assailed Gnosticism, Sabellianism and moral laxity with vigour. In the vast extent of his literary work and his immense erudition he can be compared with Origen. The numerous versions of his works, Latin, Syriac, Coptic, Arabic, Ethiopic, Georgian, Slavonian show what his reputation was in the East. His influence on his successors and on Origen has yet to be fully estimated.

Writings. Polemical. *Philosophumena*, or *Refutation of all heresies* (kata pason haireseon elenchos) (228-233), in ten books, is called the Labyrinth by Photius. In the preface he

81

says his purpose is to teach heretics that they are dependent not on Scripture but on Greek philosophy for their teaching. In Books 1-4 he aims at setting forth the teaching of pagan philosophers (hence the name) and then to show that heretics simply carry on their teaching. Book 10 sums up. Book 9, dealing with Modalism, is ruined by prejudice, accounts of quarrels with Zephyrinus and Callistus.

The next work *Syntagma* or 'Adversus omnes haereses', (post 200) treats of thirty-two heresies, the last being that of Noetus. Epiphanius and others used this work. It was composed while Zephyrinus (199-217) still lived.

Exegetical and Controversial. (A) His scriptural writings are his best. Like Origen he was first an exegete, brilliant if not as profound as Origen. Most of his attention was devoted to Genesis. Unlike Origen he took the historical meaning chiefly. He was, however, a great lover of allegory. (a) *Treatise on Anti-Christ* (c. 200), the only dogmatic treatise to survive complete, in Greek. (b) *Commentary on Daniel* (204) is still extant and the earliest known commentary on Scripture. (c) *Commentary on the Canticle of Canticles* – extant largely. *Fragments* of works on Proverbs, Ecclesiastes, Zacharias, Genesis, Numbers, Deuteronomy, Kings, Psalms, Isaias, Ezechiel. He does not proceed word by word but deals with the ideas in these books.

(B) His zeal for the faith led him to attack every form of error. (1) *Against the Greeks and against Plato*; (2) *Against the Jews*; (3) *Against Marcion:* (Gnostics); (4) Concerning *Charismata*, (if distinct from 'Apostolic Tradition' below), against Montanists; (5) Against the rabid *anti-Montanists*, e.g. Caius; (6) Against the *Modalists* (Noetus) and *Adoptianists*, *Against Artemon*.

Dogmatic Works. *Treatise on Anti-Christ* (above); on God and the *Resurrection* of the Body; *Exhortation to Severina*; *On the Economy* (Incarnation).

Historical Chronicles – a historical and geographical compilation aimed at harmonising the Bible and profane history. (Cf. Julius Africanus), after 234. A few Greek Fragments and some re-written Latin passages remain. Easter Cycle, (determing the date of Easter) beginning with A.D. 222. *Liturgy* and *Canon Law*. He may have composed a disciplinary work of which two writings on the necessity of fasting on Saturdays and of daily communion (cf. St. Jerome, Ep. 71, 7) formed part.

The *Apostolic Tradition* (c. 215) (inscribed on the statue) was

82

already known and from 1891 was called the *Egyptian Church Order* because it was known only in Ethiopic and Coptic translations. There are also Latin and Arabic versions. It is of immense importance and interest, giving us, as Quasten says, 'a new foundation for the history of the Roman Liturgy, and the richest source of information that we possess in any form for our knowledge of the constitution and life of the Church in the first three centuries'. In 1910 E. Schwarz claimed the work as that of Hippolytus and after considerable controversy R. H. Connolly, OSB, in 1916 showed (1) that all the disciplinnary works like the *Order* are subsequent to and derived from it; (2) that this *Order* is substantially Hippolytus's *Apostolic Tradition*. So the *Canones Hippolyti* 112 and *Constitutions per Hippolytum* 113 cannot in their present form be his.

The *Apostolic Tradition* contains the earliest ritual of ordination that we possess and it is Roman. There are long liturgical excerpts – it gives a list of ordinations of bishops, priests and deacons and 'speaks of confessors, widows, readers, virgins, subdeacons, catechumens, offices and prayer, baptism, fasting, the agape, first fruits, Easter fast, Eucharist, time of prayer'. Regarding penance, alleged reservation of certain sins and impossibility of forgiving them, and similar problems arising out of Hippolytus's writings, it may be surmised with Rossi and d'Ales 'that during the pontificate of Callistus a certain softening down of discipline in particular cases took place; and that his enemies probably resented his extremely discreet innovations in disciplinary matters much less than they did his energy in dogmatically affirming the Church's unrestricted right of granting pardon'. Funk (1907) says: 'In a lesser degree even that Tertullian, can Hippolytus be quoted to prove that the Roman Church, prior to Callistus, held that the three sins of impudicitia, murder and idolatry were absolutely unpardonable both in theory and in practice'.

CHURCH ORDERS

The *Apostolic Constitutions (Canones ecclesiastici apostolorum)*, compiled in Syria about 380, depends on Hippolytus's work and is the most important collection of liturgical laws that has come down from Christian antiquity. It was published first in Venice in 1563. Books 1-6 reproduce the *Didascalia* almost literally. Book 7 in the first part gives a development of the *Didache* and in the second part contains prayers and directions for catechumens and baptism. A morning prayer contains almost entirely the *Gloria* of the Mass. Book 8 is the most valuable book, and has as source the 'Constitutions of Hippolytus', it contains, *inter alia*, the whole liturgy of the 'Clementine' Mass, the most complete ancient Mass we possess. There are directions for confessors, virgins, widows, exorcists, proselytes, and chapter 47 gives eighty-five *Canones Apostolici (infra)*. Author was probably an Arian. Constantinople is also possible as place of origin.

There is also an Epitome of this Book 8 which is in fact not an abbreviation but a series of excerpts, and drew independently on Hippolytus's *Apostolic Tradition*; it goes also under the name of *Constitutiones per Hippolytum*.

Canones Apostolici, composed probably by the author of the *Apostolic Constitutions*, is concerned almost entirely with the choice, ordination and duties of clerics.

The Testament of Our Lord contains two books in Greek and we know it only through versions – Syriac, Coptic, Ethiopic, Arabic. It is an elaboration of Hippolytus's *Apostolic Tradition*. It was printed for the first time 1899. Probably fifth century, Syria.

Canons of Hippolytus, probably about A.D. 500, depends on the *Tradition* also. Extant in Arabic and Ethiopic versions.

NOVATIAN

Novatian has already been referred to in treating of St. Cyprian. He was a distinguished member of the Roman clergy up to 251 and two letters from them to Cyprian were written by him, after Pope Fabian's death (20 Jan. 250). In 251, as a rigorist, he opposed Pope Cornelius, and demanded that the lapsi of the Decian persecution be refused re-admittance to the Church. Like Hippolytus, he headed a schism, became anti-pope, but did not withdraw, and his schism spread and lasted for many centuries (to the sixth). We know nothing of his death.

Writings. St. Cyprian and St. Jerome, are sources of our information. St. Cyprian depicts him as a harsh, unyielding, unmerciful rigorist. These two and Pope Cornelius admit, and his two letters testify to, his superior ability as a rhetorician and a philosopher. (1) *Letters.* (2) *De Trinitate* (c. 250) is remarkable considering its date. It treats of God the Father, the Son, (his divinity and humanity) and the Holy Ghost, and with great ability. (3) *De Cibis Judaicis* – addressed to the Novatian community at Rome, shows that certain foods were forbidden to the Jews but that Christians, apart from the precept of temperance, are bound only to avoid meats offered to idols. Occasional reminiscences of Seneca are noteworthy. *De Spectaculis*, and *De Bono Pudicitiae* are probably his, also.

COMMODIAN. VICTORINUS OF PETTAU. RETICIUS OF AUTUN. ACTA MARTYRUM

Commodian. His life is known from his own writings. He is the first Christian Latin poet. Born a heathen, he became a Christian and he lived in the Latin West (born possibly at Gaza in Palestine). His works were written c. 250.

Writings. *Instructions.* Two books of poems (1) against Jews and heathens; (2) urges Christians to fulfil their duties. and avoid sin. The metre is hexameter. All the poems are acrostic, i.e. the initial letters of successive verses express the theme and title of the poem. *Carmen Apologeticum* is like *Instructions*, has 1,060 lines, introduction (1-88) – nature of God, Redemption, the Saviour; significance of names of Fathers and Son; stern warning to heathens, Jews – stirring description of Last Judgment. The metre is hexameter. The literary form is unattractive, and the author is guilty of a gross form of Chiliasm. 'The content of his writings betrays a practical and sagacious ecclesiastic, filled with benevolent zeal, but endowed with slight theological culture'.

Victorinus of Pettau, earliest exegete of the Latin Church, bishop of Pettau, was martyred in the Diocletian persecution. He wrote several commentaries and showed himself a disciple of Origen. We know only his work on the Apocalypse.

Reticius of Autun, in the reign of Constantine, bishop of Autun (city of the Aedui), was highly esteemed in Gaul. He wrote on the Canticle of Canticles, and against Novatian. 'While the diction of the commentary was choice and pleasing, it contained many singular and foolish opinions'.

Acta Martyrum. From very early times the anniversary of a martyr's death was celebrated with a liturgical service, and a narrative of the events was read. Eusebius made a collection of *Acta Martyrum.* They were of three kinds: (1) official documents – *acta gesta* – and by official notaries. These are valuable, e.g. *Acta Cypriani Proconsularia*, (2) Narratives of witnesses – *passiones*, – lacking in official authenticity but valuable. (3) Later accounts, embellished, sometimes figments. *(Martyrium S. Polycarpi, Acta SS. Carpi, Papyli et Agathonices*, (160-180); *Acta S. Justini et Sociorum* (163-167); *Acta Mm. Scillitanorum* (17 July 180); *Acta S. Apollonii* (180-192); *Acta SS. Perpetuae et Felicitatis* (202): *Acta S. Cipriani* (258).

THE SECOND PERIOD
THE GOLDEN AGE OF PATRISTIC LITERATURE
(Saec. IV-V)

FIRST SECTION: GREEK WRITERS

General conspectus; Arianism; Macedonianism; Sabellianism, Apollinarism.

Eusebius of Caesarea
 (c. 263-340)
Egyptian Monachism
St. Cyril of Jerusalem
 (c. 315-386)
St. Gregory of Nazianzus
 (c. 329-390)
Didymus the Blind († 398)
Diodore of Tarsus
 († c. 393)
St. John Chrysostom
 (354-407)
Theodoret of Cyrus
 (c. 393-458)
St. John Damascene
 (c. 675-c. 749)

St. Athanasius
 (c. 295-373)
Anti-Manichaean writers
St. Basil the Great
 (329-379)
St. Gregory of Nyssa
 (c. 335-c. 394)
St. Epiphanius (c. 315-403)
Theodore of Mopsuestia
 († 428)
St. Cyril of Alexandria
 (?-444)
Other writers and works

SECOND SECTION: SYRIAC WRITERS

Introduction
St. Ephraem Syrus (306-373)

Aphraates (+367)
Later writers

THIRD SECTION: LATIN WRITERS

General Conspectus.
Firmicius Maternus
 † (post 360)
Other Anti-Arian writers
Schism, heresies – defenders and opponents

St. Hilary of Poitiers
 (c. 310-367)

St. Ambrose (c. 339-397)	Poets and Historians
	Prudentius (348-post 405),
St. Sulpicius Severus	and Paulinus († 431)
(† c. 420);	St. Jerome (349?-420)
Tyrannius Rufinus	Gallic writers
(c. 345-410)	Writings of St. Patrick
St. Augustine (354-430)	(fl. 432-461?)

Pope St. Leo the Great (440-461) and other Italian writers
Pope St. Gregory the Great (c. 540-504)

THE GOLDEN AGE OF PATRISTIC LITERATURE

Introduction and general conspectus

The period which stretches from St. Athanasius to the death of St. Augustine is the golden age of patristic literature, producing as it did the most talented and prolific writers. It saw the rise of Arianism and Pelagianism and the beginning of the Christological disputes; Arianism, condemned in 325, is defeated by St. Athanasius and St. Hilary. In the second part (360-430) we meet the Cappadocian Fathers, St. Basil, St. Gregory Nazianzenus and St. Gregory of Nyssa; St. John Chrysostom (of Antioch school); in the West, St. Jerome, St. Ambrose, St. Augustine – to name only the most outstanding writers. So far the Church had been struggling for her existence against persecution, and Church writers were concerned with the defence of the Church. The edict of toleration of January 313 gave peace to the Church and tolerated Christianity as a *religio licita, (lawful religion)*. It was only a short step to the overthrow of paganism, and in 337 Constantine was baptized and his sons assumed a hostile attitude to heathenism and Christianity became the State religion under Theodosius. An attempt by Julian the Apostate (361-363) to infuse life into the old paganism failed. In 392 the worship of the gods was declared treason, and by 423 heathenism was looked on in the East as defunct.

Peace ushered in a new era in Christian literature. The writers could now afford to concern themselves solely with domestic matters. The *conversion of the educated classes* in the empire gave the Church eminent scholars and orators, and men of culture. Men were able to spend more time at study and undertake lengthy works. The *great heresies* provided a powerful stimulus to literary activity. Lastly the *development of the monastic life* with its solitude, silence and prayer gave great depth and solidity to the works of many of the Fathers. As a result of these influences the great authors of this period present Christian truths in classical style; they combine the findings of philosophy admirably with the faith; they write on almost everything with brilliance – exegesis, apologetics, controversy, dogmatic and moral theology, asceticism, poetry, etc. *Advantages* of the State preference for Christianity besides those enumerated were: the clergy soon developed into an independent body in pursuit of their ministry; the higher prelates received considerable political privileges; ecclesiastical councils were more frequently held and with great solemcity. *Drawbacks* conterbalanced these somewhat: *Caesaropapism* was a serious menace especially when the civil power supported Arianism. The clergy often became very subservient to the court and their obsequiousness postponed the defeat of Arianism for many years. The *breaking-up of the empire* aggravated these evils. Diocletian divided the empire into east and west. Constantine restored the monarchy in 323, after the defeat of Licinius, but this did not arrest the tendency, nor did Theodosius's establishment of unity have lasting results. The first step led to an inevitable separation. The result was serious for the Church, because many members of the episcopate in the East (chiefly Arian) thought of Church in terms of State. The sense of Christian unity was blunted by this division.

(a) **Development of Doctrine.** Only a summary outline can be given here as the questions belong to Church History and Dogmatic Theology. They centre round Christ's Person. 'It is the development and determination of ecclesiastical doctrine that lend to this epoch its distinct character. To the East particularly falls the special task of abstract crystallisation and speculative illustration of theological truths in their strict significance'. 'The true divinity and perfect humanity of Christ are established against Arianism, Macedonianism, Sabellianism and Apollinarism (Conc. Constantinople, 381). The relation of the human and the divine in the God-Man is defined to mean that two natures are united in one person, but without confusion and without change'. (Bardenhewer).

(b) **Heresies.** In the fourth century there were at least ten kinds of heresies.

(A) The first five concern the Trinity or Christology.

89

(1) **Arians.** Arius, a priest of Alexandria, taught that the Logos was a creature created ex nihilo, from nothing, before the creation of the world, by nature distinct from the Father; he is the Son of God as all men are sons of God, by adoption. The second creature was the Holy Ghost. The Father alone is true God. Nicaea (325) condémned this and taught the Son of God was of the same substance or nature as the Father *(homoousios to Patri)*. There were extremists and moderates. Emperors sponsored it freely. It lasted on into the ninth century. St. Athanasius, St. Basil, St. Gregory of Nazianzus and St. Gregory of Nyssa were the great Church representatives.

2. **Pneumatomachi** denied the divinity of the Holy Ghost and so the Trinity. Their heresy comes from Arianism and they are called Semi-Arians, Macedonians, Marathonians, (Tropicists).

3. **Sabellians** *(supra)* held the divine persons were only modes or modalities of the same Person, God. They are called Photinians (Photinus, bishop of Sirmium). They believed there was only a modal distinction – God as Creator, Redeemer, Sanctifier. A logical outcome of it was *Patripassianism.* Marcellus, bishop of Ancyra (-374) is associated with Sabellianism, his aim being to emphasise the unity of nature of Father and Son and he suppressed the distinction of persons. Eusebius and Athanasius opposed it.

4. **Apollinarists** (Apollinaris, 390, bishop of Laodicea, Syria), to render Christ's divinity more certain, taught his humanity was incomplete – a body and a sensitive soul. The word took the place of the spiritual soul. Apollinaris was 'one of the most fertile and versatile ecclesiastical writers of his time – primarily an exegete'.

5. **Nestorians** denied the personal unity of Christ – taught two separate persons in Him and so denied the God-Man. The heresy did not come to a head until 430.

(B) 1. The **Origenists** defended Origen's eschatological errors and the temporal nature of hell. (There was a prudent Origenism which favoured a spiritual exegesis – not to be confused with above).

2. **Manichaeans** taught two eternal and irreducible principles, *good* and *evil*, and advanced this as an explanation of all natural and supernatural mysteries.

3. **Donatists** led by Donatus of Carthage affirmed the saints and the just form the Church and taught that the validity of the sacraments depends on the holiness of the minister.

90

4. **Pelagians** taught that the human will was all powerful in the moral order, and denied the need of grace to move it.

5. **Priscillianists** taught a doctrine which combined Sabellianism, Manichaeism and some Origenist theories. .

These heresies were opposed by individual Fathers and by group movements in schools of theology in the East.

(A) **The School of Alexandria** – Clement, Origen and others.
The new school flourished in the fourth century. It had for its
representatives St. Athanasius and Didymus the Blind in
Egypt, and later the Cappadocians. The school is distinctive in
its mystical interpretation and tendency, and employment of
Platonic philosophy. 'In theology their faith in the divinity of
the Word led them to a clear affirmation of His substantial
sameness with the Father'. They readily accepted the *homo-
ousios* of Nicaea. The unity of God was first in their thought,
and this they stressed though enemies might accuse them of
Sabellianism. 'The Alexandrians became the defenders of the
substantial and personal unity of Christ', and so strenuously
that Monophysitism sought to claim St. Cyril as a supporter.

(B) **The School of Antioch** had three periods:

(a) 260-360. Lucianus and Dorotheus were prominent.

(b) 360-430, its great period – Flavian, Diodorus of Tarsus,
Theodore of Mopsuestia, Theodoret of Cyrus, and above all
St. John Chrysostom.

(c) The period of decadence after 430.

Characteristics of the School. The school opposed to the
allegorical interpretation of Alexandria a prudent, literal sense,
either proper or metaphorical, insisting on the helps afforded
by language-study, etc. Occasionally the spirit was neglected
for the letter. For the mystical they substituted a moral
teaching (especially St. Chrysostom). They cultivated Aristotelian philosophy. In theology they affirmed clearly the
distinction of the divine Persons and to ensure the reality of
the distinction gave them the name of hypostases (*hypostasis*,
substance) thereby risking the possibility of being accused of
holding the theory that the Persons are not only a substance
but differ from one another by a substance. For this reason
many of them opposed *homo-ousios*, and the misuse of the
word by Paul of Samosata in the previous century helped them
to this. The school stressed the *humanity* of Christ in its
Christology. The later heresies centred principally on the
person of Christ – was He true God and true Man? How many
persons in Christ? Errors often arose from a too zealous
defence of orthodoxy in one point. Nestorius was combating

the loss of human will in Christ and held there were two persons in Christ. Under stress of these heresies and questionings theology developed with great precision, and an elaborate and systematic defence of Christianity resulted (especially concerning the Incarnation and Redemption).

(C) In the fourth century there are writers who belong to a movement which may be classed as the **Traditional School.** It can be observed first in reaction to Origen, and later on rejected all scientific knowledge and criticism. In the third century Methodius had protested against certain theses of Origen, but the fourth century opposition, headed by St. Epiphanius, is more personal than scientific opposition and it frequently stooped to the use of unworthy means.

EUSEBIUS OF CAESAREA

Eusebius of Caesarea (c. 265-c. 340). He was born within ten years of Origen's death, in Caesarea, Palestine, was trained there, and enjoyed the friendship of a distinguished priest, Pamphilus, whose name he took as a mark of gratitude (Eusebius Pamphili). When Pamphilus was imprisoned, Eusebius accompanied him and worked with him at an Apology for Origen. Eusebius fled to Tyre and thence to Egypt and at the end of the persecution returned in 313 to Caesarea, and became its bishop; and enjoying Constantine's friendship was a very influential one. Despite fine qualities he laboured under serious defects, inability to grasp clearly the issues at stake in the Trinitarian controversy, a lack of independence and clear thought, readiness to make peace almost at any cost, to compromise. He believed that St. Athanasius's doctrine of homo-ousios led to Sabellianism and he was ever being more attracted to Arianism. He wanted to be conciliatory at Nicaea and it was at the Emperor's express wish he signed the profession of faith. Never in his writings before or after 325 does he use *homo-ousios*. He was prominent in the Council of Antioch which deposed its bishop, Eusebius (opponent of Arianism), (330) and in the Synod of Tyre (335) which deposed Athanasius. Chronologically he belongs to the Golden Age, but it has been said of him with truth that he is more in the spirit of the third century and occupied like the third century writers more with ideas than their artistic expression. His literary activity was many-sided.

(A) **Historical Works.** None of his works met with such unqualified approval from the beginning as his 'Chronicle' and 'Church History', and his work in this sphere has earned for him the title of the 'Christian Herodotus' and 'Father of Church History'.

(1) **Chronicle** (Divers Histories – *Epitome Pantodapes Historias*) is divided into two parts. The first part aims at giving a chronological account of the outstanding events of each nation, the second part at giving a synchronisation and co-ordination of these happenings. St. Jerome translated the second part into Latin. Julius Africanus had attempted something similar. Throughout Eusebius's work there runs the idea that remote history and the history of his own time are closely connected and the influence of such a view on later historiography is incalculable. 'The second part... presents a page with columns of dates down its central portion, assembled according to various systems of chronology, those columns being flanked to the right and left by columns of sacred and profane history. Nothing could be more unattractive in appearance than these bald synchronised annals, and yet they are the mode for the chronicles, universal and local, which are in fashion for a thousand years in the West. They present a scheme of ancient chronology which has been accepted almost unaltered down to our day. They marshal the whole panorama of ancient history to show that it was but a preparation for the gospel – a magnificent synthesis, implying an erudition and judgment which are the admiration of modern historians, and a great conception inherited from Origen and presented here with the simplicity and clarity of a mathematical curve'. (Campbell)

(2) **The Church History** is a collection of facts and documents and excerpts from a multitude of writings belonging to the early years of the Church. It described the life of the Church from earliest times down to Constantine's victory (313), in nine books, and a tenth was later added to cover the period to 323 (defeat of Licinius and sole rulership of Constantine). It is a priceless treasure in view of the ruin and loss of so much literature before it – its value is beyond calculation. In the most literal sense it is a source-book, our only source for various documents. Eusebius had prejudices in favour of Constantine, but apart from that he is a reliable historian. He reveals, generally speaking, charity (in the Arian struggle) 'and in the management of vast reserves of learning a conscientious striving for accuracy and detachment. It presents world-

94

history since the founding of the Church as an unceasing battle between the devil and the kingdom of God; the events of history are so many manifestations of the will of God for His world. By this work... he is best known to after times. Through it and the Chronicle Eusebius enjoys an influence in the after-world surpassed only by Origen, Chrysostom, and possibly the Areopagite among the Greek Fathers'. (Campbell).

(B) **Exegetical Works.** In these he follows Origen. His commentaries are practically all lost. Fragments of those on the New Testament (St. Luke especially) have reached us. He wrote a kind of Gospel Harmony also.

(C) **Apologetic Works.** He frequently defended Christian truth and always with success, due mainly to his grasp of history.

(1) *Evangelical Preparation* (15 books) shows the superiority of Christianity and even of Judaism over all heathen systems.

(2) *Evangelical Demonstration* (20 books) shows that Christianity is the divine development of Judaism (10 books have reached us). He abridged these two works in five books 'On the appearance of God among men'.

(D) **Doctrinal Works.** (a) Two books, Against Marcellus (of Ancyra) to prove he was rightly deposed by the Arians in 336 (for Sabellianism); (b) three books, *On Ecclesiastical Theology* expound and defend the true doctrine of the Logos.

ST. ATHANASIUS

St. Athanasius, Doctor of the Church, (c. 295-373) was born in Alexandria and was bishop there for nearly half a century, where he earned for himself the title 'The Great' and the reputation for all time as the intrepid and brilliant defender of the faith against Arianism. His extensive writings – exegetical, apologetical, dogmatic, disciplinary, moral, polemical – are all concerned with the dominant purpose and idea in his life – the defence of the divinity of Christ. The 'pillar of the Church' (St. Gregory of Nazianus) and the 'God-given physician of her wounds' (St. Basil), he is one of the most imposing figures of ecclesiastical history. Alexander, the bishop of Alexandria, was much impressed by the young Athanasius, and St. Anthony directed the youth's life for a time. In 319 Athanasius was made deacon and secretary and counsellor to the bishop whom he accompanied to Nicaea (325) where he proved a powerful opponent of Arianism. He was chosen as successor to Alexander on the latter's death (17 April 328) and the remainder of his life he spent between struggles for the faith, brief periods of quiet, synods, banishments, battles with bishops and magistrates and emperors. The Arians condemned and deposed him at Tyre (335) and he was banished by Constantine to Trier. He returned in 338 on Constantine's death. Condemned at Antioch (339) he went to Rome to Pope Julius. Constantius sided with the Arians and Arian Pistus, and afterwards George of Cappadocia seized the see of Alexandria by force. Julius declared Athanasius innocent and the Synod of Sardica declared him the rightful occupant of the see of Alexandria (343). Only in 346 could he return.

After the death of his brother Constans (350), Constantius supported the Arians again and the Synod of Arles (353) and Milan (355) deposed Athanasius. George entered Alexandria again while Athanasius went to the monks in Egypt. Julian (362) recalled banished bishops but Athanasius was banished again in the same year as a disturber. Jovian (363-364) allowed him to return – his successor Valens (Arian) banished him – now for the fifth time. After four months he allowed him to return and having spent seventeen years out of his see, he lived now in peace until his death, 2 May 373.

Writings

(A) **Apologetic** (*Oratio Contra Gentes*, 2 books). (a) Against the emptiness of pagan pantheism, it shows the reasonableness and necessity of Christianity; (b) *Oratio de incarnatione Verbi* (against pagans and Jews). About A.D. 320.

(B) **Dogmatic Works** are almost all against the Arians:

(1) *Orationes contra Arianos IV*, is the longest and most important work. B. I teaches the eternal origin of the Son from the Father and the substantial unity of both. Bks. 3 and 4 gives an explanation of the pertinent texts of Scripture, and Bk. IV deals with the personal distinction of the Son from the Father. This was written in Egypt about 356-362 (third exile). (2) *Letters IV to Serapion*, bishop of Thmuis, refuting the theory of those who, admitting the divinity of the Son, maintained that the Holy Ghost is a creature. (3) *Liber de Trinitate et de Spiritu Sancto* (c. 365) extant only in Latin (ranked *inter spuria* by some). (4) *Epistola encyclica ad episcopos* (340); (5) *Epistola ad Antiochenos*; (6) *Ep. ad Jovinianum imperatorem* (363); (7) *Ep. encyclica ad episcopos Aegypti et Libyae*, (356-361); (8) *Ep. ad Epictetum* (c. 371) – bishop òf Corinth – about

Christological doctrine; Ep. ad Adelphium, (Letter to Adelphius;) Ep. ad Maximum, (Letter to Maximus). These three were important, especially 'to Epictetus'. The Nestorians interpolated it and were convicted of the fraud by St. Cyril of Alexandria.

(C) **Historico-Polemical Writings.** He wrote three Apologies to justify his conduct; (1) *Apology against the Arians*, 350 – very important for history; (2) *Apology to the Emperor Constantius*, 356; (3) *Apology for his flight*, 357. Two encyclical letters might be classed here too, i.e. numbers 4 and 7 above. There are letters on the decrees of Nicaea; on the doctrine of Dionysius, bishop of Alexandria (350); letter to monks, called *Historia Arianorum*, letter (359) on the proceedings of the Councils of Rimini and Seleucia; letter (two) to Lucifer, bishop of Cagliari (360).

(D) **Exegetical Writings.** We have only fragments of these in Catenae, the most important of them belonging to a commentary on the Psalms. Allegorical interpretation is in evidence.

(E) **Ascetical.** In 357 (365?) Athanasius composed a **biography of St. Anthony** as the model of the dedicated life. Evagrius of Antioch translated it into Latin and it helped greatly in East and West to arouse enthusiasm for the ascetic and monastic life. Athanasius had spent some time with monks himself.

(F) **Festal Letters.** It was an ancient custom for bishops of Alexandria to send Festal Letters after Epiphany to their churches announcing the date of Easter and of the preparatory fast and instructions about the Easter festival etc. In 1857 a collection in Syriac of some sent by Athanasius was found in a monastery of the Nitrian desert and Cureton edited them in 1848 – they are for the years 329-348 and contain fifteen letters. These are valuable for the history of Arianism.

Teaching on Christ is contained in his phrase 'God became man in order to deify men'. Christ is true God and true man. God is a unity, but in this unity is included a trinity. The name Father supposes the existence of a Son. The Son is not from nothing, nor from the will of the Father, but from the substance of the Father; He is co-eternal with the Father, shares with Him the entire plenitude of the divinity. Father and Son are two but their nature is one. The Spirit of God shares the same divinity and the same power. The source of the Holy Spirit is the Son who is with the Father. He is of one and the same substance with the Father and the Son. There is, thus, but one divinity and one God in three persons.

97

The menace that Arianism was cannot be exaggerated. We cannot now easily picture the details of the struggle, we are too solidly established in the security of doctrine which men like Athanasius expounded and vindicated. There is no struggle against heresy that can be cited as a parallel to it, for it was a matter of life or death for the Christian religion. The mystery of the Trinity, the divinity of the Son and the Holy Ghost are at the heart of Christianity. If Christ, as Arians, maintained, was a creature, then we were not redeemed, the new and complete revelation has not been made, worship of Christ is idolatry.

Athanasius's greatness lies in his victory over Arianism. 'He was the chief instrument, his was the major role, in that conflict which determined that Christianity was to continue... Great minds and greater literary artists fight in the ranks of orthodoxy, but Athanasius is the leader of them all and the personal inspiration of most'. For the Christian philosopher, however much he may wish to draw on reason and its findings, the goal is predetermined – there is Revelation and between it and reason there can be no clash. St. Athanasius 'is the first clear manifestation to us moderns of how Revelation must act when forced by an intellectual crisis to be specific. To have been the leading protagonist of Revelation in such a crisis as was Arianism... was to live a career of sovereign importance to the future of civilisation' (Campbell).

The Athanasian Creed known also as 'Quicunque vult' was not composed by St. Athanasius; the attribution to him, accepted from seventh century, has been abandoned since the researches of G. Voss (1642), chiefly on the ground that the Creed contains doctrinal expressions that envisage controversies. Because of its clear expression of the doctrine of the Trinity and Incarnation, formulated in forty rhythmical propositions, it was universally accepted and until recently was recited in Prime on many Sundays of the year. Since the seventeenth century it has been recognised that it was composed later than St. Athanasius's time and in Latin, and until fairly modern times it circulated only in the West. It has been ascribed to: St. Vincent of Lerins (450), St. Hilary of Arles (449), Fulgentius of Ruspe, North Africa (533), Caesarius o Arles (542), etc. The doctrines defended and the terminology used suggest a time when Apollinarism was a danger and before Nestorianism and Eutychianism (which are not referred to). Probably it was written between 381 and 428. The precise

98

date and authorship must remain yet open matters, but the thesis of H. Brewers, S.J. (1909) has received very wide acceptance: St. Ambrose was the author, and 382/3 the date.

EGYPTIAN MONACHISM

St. Anthony (cf. St. Athanasius's biography) is reputed to be the founder of the cenobitic life. He died in 356, on Mt. Colzim near the Red Sea, aged 105.

St. Pachomius was the first legislator of the monks. Tabennisi, north of Thebes, on the right bank of the Nile, was the scene of his labours. He died in 345 or 346. Other representatives: St. Orsisius, St. Theodorus, SS. Macarius the Egyptian and Macarius the Alexandrine.

Anti-Manichaean Writers. Towards the end of the third century Manichaeism began to appear in the Graeco-Roman world. Christian authors who wrote against it were Hegemonius, Alexander of Lycopolis, St. Serapion of Thmuis, Titus of Bostra. (Also St. Basil, Didymus, Diodorus of Tarsus.)

ST. CYRIL OF JERUSALEM

St. Cyril of Jerusalem, Doctor of the Church, (c. 313-386), was born probably in Palestine and educated at Jerusalem. In 325 he was ordained deacon, and Maximus II ordained him priest in 345, and as priest, probably in 347, he delivered the famous Catecheses, catechetical instructions to the candidates for baptism and the neophytes. When Maximus died, Cyril was consecrated bishop of Jerusalem (348-350). He did not engage in doctrinal controversies though in his Catecheses he opposed Arianism but without mentioning it or *homo-ousios*. He was troubled greatly later by the Arians and the ostensible reason was a dispute about the primacy of honour granted to Jerusalem by Can. 7 of Nicaea without prejudice to the metropolitan rights of Caesarea. He was expelled three times from his see, 357, 360 and 367. Caesarea accused him to the Synod of Seleucia (361) reinstated him but the Synod of Constantinople (362) deposed him. In 361 Julian recalled all bishops and he returned. At this time occurred the phenomenon of fire falling on the workers who were engaged on the rebuilding of the Temple. Cyril had assured his people that the work would not succeed. Ammianus Marcellinus, a pagan author, confirms the story. Valens deposed Cyril in 367 and eleven years later on Valens's death (378) Cyril returned and had peace for his remaining years. He attended the second General Council (381) where he at last confessed *homo-ousios* verbally and died in 386, 18 March.

The Catecheses are twenty-three (24, if the first, introduction, is counted) in number, and contain a complete body of doctrine. Their authenticity was never questioned in ancient times. The first eighteen (19) were addressed to candidates for baptism *(photizomenoi, those being enlightened)* and delivered during Lent in the great basilica of Constantine built on the side of the hill of Calvary. Numbers 1-5 deal with the grace about to be bestowed, sin, penance, baptism; the outlines of the Christian faith; the nature and origin of the theological virtue of faith. Numbers 6-18 give a continuous exposition and demonstration of every word of the Creed as recited in Jerusalem. At Easter the catechumens were baptised and received Confirmation and the Blessed Eucharist, and to the new Christians *(neo-photistoi, the newly enlightened)* the remaining five lectures were delivered in the chapel of the Resurrection. These aim at making known the mysteries of Christianity *(katecheseis mustagogikai, lessons leading into the mysteries),* and give complete instructions on Baptism, Confirmation and the Blessed Eucharist. They have always been looked on as models of instruction. 'Their diction is simple and clear, and the entire exposition is mildly grave, tranquil, and cordial. Their subject-matter causes them to be looked on as one the most precious treasures of Christian antiquity; the five mystagogical catecheses, in particular, are of incalculable value for the history of doctrine and the liturgy'. (Bardenhewer). St. Cyril bears incontrovertible witness to the Real Presence of Christ in the Blessed Eucharist (Cat. 22, 9; cf. Cat. 22, 2; 23, 7); and to the reality of the Sacrifice of the Mass (23, 8-10). We have also his homily on a paralytic (345); a letter to the Emperor Constantius about the shining cross in the sky (7 May 351), and three small homiletic fragments.

ST. BASIL THE GREAT

St. Basil the Great (329-379), bishop of Caesarea, Doctor of the Church, is the first of the great Cappadocian group (St. Gregory of Nyssa, his brother; St. Gregory of Nazianzus, his friend). 'In this trinity are concentrated all the rays of that brilliant epoch of Christianity'. Born at Caesarea of noble and wealthy Christian parents, Basil was educated by his father, Basil, at Neo-Caesarea, and received higher education in Caesarea, Constantinople and Athens. Basil was not captivated by Athens, and returned home in 359, after four or five years, determined to abandon the life of fame as a rhetorician that could certainly have been his, for the monastic life. He journeyed through Syria and Egypt to study the life of the monks, returned home, distributed his goods to the poor and began a life devoted to God. He preferred the cenobitic to the hermit life. His teaching and example were so powerful that in a short time Pontus was changed. Gregory of Nazianzus came often to the Pontic desert, and he and Basil formed a rule for the monasteries that arose all around. They published a selection from Origen's works *(Philokalia)*. Eusebius, elected to Caesarea, asked Basil to help him, persuaded him to become a priest and return to Caesarea to face the difficulties created by Arianism. Eusebius was not a skilled theologian himself, and Basil was to him 'a good counsellor, a skilful helper, an expounder of the Scripture, an interpreter of his duties, ...the prop of his faith' (Greg. Naz.). During this period he wrote the *Hexaemeron* – The Six Days, Work.

Eusebius died in 370, and Basil succeeded him as metropolitan of Caesarea. He found many abuses to be corrected, including simony and laxity in ordination, and encountered a good deal of opposition to his reforms. Before his death he had brought the clergy of Caesarea to such a standard that other bishops used to ask them to help them in their dioceses. He undertook great social-relief works, established industries and schools of Art and founded orphanages, the chief one being the building of the Ptocho-tropheion, institute for the care of the poor. He had numerous clashes with the Arian emperor Valens, whom he withstood as he had withstood Julian the Apostate (a friend of his Athens days). He suffered a great deal of ill health, and the ill-will of many bishops, including his uncle Gregory, caused him considerable annoyance. In 371 Cappadocia was divided and two capitals created –

101

Caesarea and Tyana – and grievous discord was caused between Basil and Anthimus. Basil, to counteract his influence, appointed Gregory of Nazianzus bishop of the wretched frontier town of Sasima, for which Gregory never quite forgave him. He tried frequently to heal the Meletian schism at Antioch. He concerned himself above all with the overthrow of Arianism. The mantle of Athanasius fell on him, and though during the troubled years of his brief episcopate his true worth was not fully appreciated, he was soon after his death hailed as 'Great' recognised as a champion of orthodoxy second only to St. Athanasius in his controversial and expository powers. For this, and for his role as the final architect of monachism as it still obtains in the East, he is chiefly renowned. The common house, common table, common prayers which are permanent possessions in the West were welded by him into a system. 'He reduced the ascetical extravagance of eremitical enthusiasm to the abiding capacity of human nature. Through him monasticism became an institution, something that could live and grow without the capricious appeal of a great personality or the spontaneous ascetical fervour of a particular age and country'. (Campbell). He died on 1 January, 379, after nine years of hard work and bitter disappointments, quarrels and broken health and the whole population, Christian, Jew and pagan, mourned him.

Writings

(A) **Dogmatico-Polemical.** These are devoted to the overthrow of Arianism. (a) *Against Eunomius* (364) three books. Eunomius, he says, is guilty of deceit in calling his own work 'Apologeticus', whereas it is really an attack. Bk. 1 deals with the essence and attributes of God; (2) the consubstantiality of the Son; and (3) the objections of Eunomius against the divinity of the Holy Ghost. These books deal with the Trinitarian doctrine (b) *De Spiritu Sancto, The Holy Spirit* (375) treats of the consubstantiality of the Son and the Holy Spirit with the Father and defends the doxology 'Glory be to the Father with the Son together with the Holy Spirit' (maintaining it was as orthodox as 'Glory be to the Father through the Son in the Holy Spirit'). His *De Spiritu Sancto* prepared the way for the decrees which Constantinople (381) gave on the creed.

(B) **Exegetical Writings.** (1) The *Hexaemeron*, – nine homilies given by Basil as a priest before 370 (Gen. 1,1-26) – all Christian antiquity esteemed them very highly. (2) *On the Psalms* (370), sixteen homilies (number uncertain). Basil kept to the literal sense. (3) On Isaiah 1-16 – imperfect in form and contents.

(C) **Ascetical Works.** (a) A group of *Ascetica*, containing three treatises: (1) on the sublimity of the life of the monk as a soldier of Christ; (2) the excellence of the monastic life; (3) the duties of a monk. (b) *Moralia*, a group of eighty rules or instructions. Also *De Judicio Dei*, and *De Fide, Duo Sermones Ascetici*. (c) *Two monastic rules – Regulae Fusius tractatae, (the longer Rule)* and *brevius, (the shorter Rule)*. The first contains 55 longer rules, the second 313 shorter rules, both in question and answer form, setting forth the rules of the monastic life and their application to daily life. They were received universally in the East, and survive to the present day. (d) *De Baptismo*, is of doubtful origin. Rufinus translated Basil's rules into Latin.

(D) **Homilies, Letters, Liturgy.** Twenty-four homilies are accepted as genuine and they show Basil as one of the greatest pastors and orators of ecclesiastical antiquity. The most brilliant is probably his homily against usurers. The one best known, however, is the homily on the use of the pagan Classics (Migne, P.G. 31, 563-590) 'To youths as to how they shall best profit by the writings of the pagan authors'. In this he uses the illustration of the bee collecting honey from flowers while avoiding poison. The treatise became very celebrated. It certainly helped to preserve the Classics. It was much in vogue, in the early Renaissance. Twenty editions of it appeared before 1500.

Letters. These were always very highly esteemed. They show, perhaps best of all his writings, his refinement of mind, his great and sympathetic character and the perfection of his style. There are 365 and they are important for the history of Basil's period and for points of doctrine.

The so-called *Liturgy of St. Basil* survives in the Greek text and a Coptic translation. St. Basil reduced the prayers and ceremonies in Caesarea to a fixed form and order.

St. Basil the Great was great as an exponent of doctrine, a homilist, great in practical life – (Gregory of Nazianzus was the speaker and writer; Gregory of Nyssa the thinker). The Trinity is the chief subject of his dogmatic writings. He maintains God's unity against the Arians, and the Trinity of Persons against the Sabellians.

ST. GREGORY OF NAZIANZUS

St. Gregory of Nazianzus, The Theologian, Doctor of the Church, (c. 329-390). St. Gregory was born near Arianzus, of Christian parents, and educated like Basil, at home, in Caesarea (Cappadocia) and Caesarea (Palestine), Alexandria, and Athens where he renewed an acquaintance made with Basil in Caesarea He left Athens c. 360. After about twelve years he went home and occasionally spent some time with Basil in Pontus, the monastic life being his ideal even while he was a student. Probably at Christmas 361 he was ordained priest, against his will, by his father, Gregory, bishop of Nazianzus, at the insistence of the people. He fled to Pontus, returned about Easter 362 and helped his father. On his return he preached his famous Oration (2) on the *Priesthood*. Basil appointed him to Sasima, and to Nazianzus in 374 when his father died. His friendship with Basil received a severe shock over the Sasima appointment. Gregory did not remain there long (if he ever took possession of it), and soon he retired to solitude. In 372 he returned to Nazianzus to help his father again. The latter died in 374; his mother died soon afterwards and his brother Caesarius and sister Gorgonia had already died. In 375 Gregory, who had to endure great bodily sufferings, resigned the administration of Nazianzus and retired to Seleucia in Isauria. There (379) he heard with great grief the news of Basil's death. His quiet was interrupted once more by a summons to the active life.

While Valens lived, Arianism had flourished in the East and in **Constantinople** the Catholics had dwindled to an insignificant nucleus. When Gratian took over the whole empire and then handed over the East to Theodosius, a Spaniard and a Catholic, hope for Catholicism revived. Gregory was summoned to reorganise Catholic life there in 379, to defend and rehabilitate the orthodox faith. He came, and a great revival of religion began. He settled in a small private house which he turned into a church (Anastasia), and from here in the space of two years he restored the Catholic ascendancy in spite of all obstacles and perils to his life. He knew no fear, and his eloquence won everyone. St. Jerome travelled from Syria to hear him. Theodosius handed over the cathedral to him (24 Dec. 380). The Catholics insisted on having him as their bishop. He refused until the second General Council, convoked by Theodosius, 381, assembled and the Fathers acclaimed him as their bishop. He had done his best to heal the Meletian schism and failed. Some late-comers disputed his own nomination and he gladly resigned the dignity. In a magnificent address to the episcopal assembly he bade them farewell – June 381 – and retired to Nazianzus which he directed until its bishop, Eulalius, was appointed in 383, and thenceforward he lived at Arianzus, devoted to his books and to the cherished life of quiet and asceticism. He died in 389 or 390.

Works, Orations 45. **Five Theological Orations** (27-31) are the most perfect of his orations – they have won for him the title of 'Theologian' (i.e. defender of the Godhead). They were delivered in 380 in Constantinople against the Eunomians and Macedonians. He treated of the existence, nature, attributes of God; unity of nature in the three Divine Persons; divinity of the Son; replies to objections; refutation of objections against the divinity of the Holy Spirit. Other striking orations were number 2 *Apologeticus pro fuga (supra)*; *Adversus imperatorem Julianum* (c. 363) Or. 4-5; Or. 7 *In Laudem Gorgoniae*, (369-74); *Oratio funebris in Patrem*, (375, Or. 18). Or. 21 *in laude magni Athanasii*, Or. 43 *in laudem Basilii.*

Letters. 243 written between 383 and 389. They excel in style, Ep. 101 on Christological doctrine was praised highly at Ephesus (431) and Chalcedon (451).

Poems. 200 (383-389). They were propaganda against heresies, and aimed also at supplying for the loss of pagan writings that were unsuitable for Christians. *De Vita Sua* is an outstanding one, describing the vicissitudes of his life and defending his actions.

Character. Events and the entreaties of his friends called him to an active life while he yearned for solitude. His powerful eloquence was the chief source of his success. He is one of the great Fathers, and one of the greatest orators of Christian antiquity – he has even been compared to Demosthenes. 'In his didactic discourses he appears as an exponent and defender of the tradition of Christian faith'. Not as great a ruler as Basil, he surpasses him in his command of rhetoric. Not as profound a thinker as Gregory of Nyssa, he was, more than he, the representative of the common faith of the Greek Church towards the end of the fourth century. Rufinus says of him that his teaching in dogma was looked on with respect as a rule of Christian faith. De Broglie writes: 'In a few hours and a few pages Gregory summed up and closed the controversy of a whole century'. His Apology for his flight, really a treatise on the priesthood, was a source for such works as St. Chrysostom's *De Sacerdotio* and Pope Gregory's *Regula Pastoralis*.

ST. GREGORY OF NYSSA

St. Gregory of Nyssa, Doctor of the Church, (c. 335-c. 394), was a younger brother of St. Basil who took charge of his early education. He became a teacher of rhetoric, married, but finally, after the death of his wife, entreated by friends (Greg. Naz.) he became a priest. He retired to solitude, and much against his will was consecrated bishop of an obscure place, Nyssa, under Basil's jurisdiction, in 371. In 375, due to Arian opposition, he was deposed and led a wandering life for a time, and, on the death of Valens in 378, returned in triumph to his see in 379. He attended at the Synod of Antioch (379) and Constantinople (381) where he was one of the principal theologians. He preached the funeral oration for Meletius of Antioch (381) and also in 385 and 386 for Flaccilla and Pulcheria, the wife and daughter of Theodosius. After the Synod of Constantinople (394) he is not heard of again and probably died soon after.

Writings. His life was comparatively uneventful, and it is in his writings the chief interest lies, and though he wrote on questions of orthodoxy the main interest is in his mysticism, and in the philosophical and speculative side of his work. He was a fervent disciple of Origen, some of whose errors he adopted (e.g. apokatastasis, the re-establishment of all things in God at the end of time, the doctrine that all will be saved). He was one of the most versatile writers of his day, and was especially brilliant at exegesis.

(1) **Exegetical.** Admirer of Origen, he followed his principles of allegorical interpretation (a) *De hominis opificio* and *Explicatio apologetica in Hexaemeron* (379). Both were written at the request of Peter (his brother), bishop of Sebaste, to complete Basil's homilies. (b) *De vita Moysis* (390) – on spiritual progress. (c) *De Pythonissa*, on 1 Kings 28, 12 ff. (d) *In Psalmos inscriptiones*, (e) *In Ecclesiasten*, – 8 homilies. (f) *In Canticum Canticorum homiliae XV*, God the bridegroom, the soul the bride. (g) *De beatitudinibus* – *homiliae* 8. (h) *De oratione dominica*, – *homiliae 5*.

(2) **Dogmatic.** (a) *Adversus Eunomium*, – 12 books (381).

106

Basil had attacked Eunomius – he replied after Basil's death, in five books, and Gregory replied to him. (b) *The great Catechism* – the most important work, and argumentative defence of the principal Christian doctrines against heathens, Jews and heretics. A very precious work, it aims at instructing teachers how best to seize the opponent's argument and point of view and proceed from his admission. It treats of the fundamental doctrines – Trinitarian, Christological, Soteriological, sacramental. (c) *Adversus Apollinarem* (c. 385) and *Antirrheticus*. (d) Trinitarian doctrine is dealt with in *Ad Eustathium de S. Trinitate*; *Ad Alabium*, 'That there are not Three Gods'; *Adv. Graecos ex communibus notionibus*; *Ad Simplicium de fide*. (e) *De Anima et Resurrectione*, a dialogue of Gregory with his sister Macrina after Basil's death. Gregory on his way home from a synod at Antioch visited her (379). She was in Pontus, the superior of a pious sisterhood devoted to God's service. Gregory found her in immediate danger of death and their conversation turned on their reunion in heaven. She voices Gregory's views on the soul, death, resurrection, and the final restoration of all things. It is called *Ta Makrinia*, and is modelled on the *Phaedo* which it excels in profound thought and eloquence. (f) *Contra fatum*, defending free will. (g) *Ad Hierium*, prefect of Cappadocia – on why God permits untimely deaths amongst children.

(3) **Ascetical.** (a) *De Virginitate* (c. 370) praises the state as one of perfection and virginity as the foundation of the virtues. (b) Similar ideas are found in smaller works. *To Harmonius. To Olympius*, etc. etc. (c) *Vita S. Macrinae* (+379).

(4) **Discourses** – partly moral, partly dogmatic, partly laudatory of saints and martyrs. They have the usual rhetorical display, ornament etc.

(5) **Letters.** 29. Two led to great controversies in the sixteenth and seventeenth centuries, numbers 3 (to Eustathia and Ambrosia) and 2 (on those who go as pilgrims to Jerusalem). The first tells of unhappy ecclesiastical conditions in Palestine, the second of abuses in pilgrimages.

St. Gregory's importance consists in his power of philosophical defence and demonstration of the Catholic faith. He was learned, a philosopher and a theologian and a mystic. The 'Star of Nyssa' closed the Trinitarian controversy. He was an unwearying defender of the divine nature, though not completely happy in his attempt to reconcile the Unity with the Trinity. He lays all stress on one point that the distinction of the three divine Persons consists in their immanent relations. The great work of the Cappadocian Fathers was to distinguish the meanings of *ousia*, (essence), and *hyspostasis* (could mean person or substance), till then confused. St. Athanasius found men quarrelling about words while really holding the same doctrine, and agreed to let each keep his terms provided the meaning was correct. There was danger in this. The Latins held one *hypostasis* or *substantia*, three *prosopa* or forms (we retain *substantia* where Greek would say essence, *ousia*). The Greeks substituted *ousia* for substance and abhorred *prosopon* (mask) as being Sabellian. Basil's final expression was one *ousia* (essence), three *hypostaseis* (persons). He and Gregory of Nyssa were determined that the difference between essence and personality would be understood and wrote freely on it. With Gregory of Nyssa the controversy ends. Gregory of Nyssa disposed of Arianism in detail in his books against Eunomius. The Second Council (381) ended the matter officially. St. Gregory of Nyssa left an important legacy to *philosophy* and *mysticism*. Our human knowledge of God – the possibility of knowing God in man's likeness to him, of knowing Him through the order and harmony of His creation interested him very greatly. 'But there is a direct mystical way for the soul which can rise above the world of sense, an intuitive knowledge, rare, extraordinary...' This latter theory of knowledge Gregory borrowed from Plotinus and Philo.' It is to be found in all Christian thinkers after him who lean towards mysticism. There were Christian mystics before St. Gregory, but he was the first who attempted a system, using the soul's reflection of the divine image as the basis of his effort'. (Campbell).

DIDYMUS THE BLIND

Didymus the Blind, born at Alexandria c. 310, was one of the most notable men of his age. He lost his sight while yet very young. President of the catechetical school of Alexandria for more than fifty years, he had amongst his disciples Rufinus and Jerome. He remained a layman and married. He died about 395. He was strongly influenced by Origen in his interpretation of Scripture and in theology. He was anathematised in later times as an Origenist, (i.e. believer in the pre-existence of the soul and the apokatastasis). His name was joined to Origen's in the fifth General Council, Constantinople 553, and the next three Councils repeated the condemnation. As a result much of his work perished. St. Jerome testified to the sound orthodoxy of his Trinitarian belief.

Writings

(a) **Dogmatic.** (1) *De Trinitate* – 3 books (381-392), very important. (2) *De Dogmatibus et contra Arianos*, 2 books. (3) *De Spiritu Sancto* – an outstanding work extant in St. Jerome's version. (4) *Contra Manichaeos*. (5) *Dialogues* 5?

(b) **Exegetical** St. Jerome mentioned many on the Old and New Testament and his commentaries on the canonical epistles are the most complete.

(c) **Lost,** (1) *Apologia for Origen's De Principiis*; (2) *Ad Philosophum*; (3) *De Incorporeo.* In his use of allegory and in his tendency to the mystical sense he is a thorough Origenist. His work *De Spiritu Sancto* is one of the best of its kind in Christian antiquity. Pt. 1 shows that the Holy Spirit is not a creature but is consubstantial with the Father and Son. In Pt. 2 he treats of the biblical texts on the Holy Spirit.

ST. EPIPHANIUS

St. Epiphanius (c. 315-403) was born of Christian parents in Palestine near Eleutheropolis, and devoted himself from his youth to the study of languages and the sacred sciences. He mastered Greek, Syria, Hebrew (Aramaic), Coptic, and knew some Latin. Hilarion exercised considerable influence over the youth of Palestine and Epiphanius was led to visit Egypt to learn about the ascetic life. He returned home and founded, c. 335, a monastery whose head he remained for thirty years. In 367 the bishops of Cyprus chose him for his learning and piety to be their metropolitan in Constantia, the ancient Salamina. Mortification in his life, sanctity, activity in the spread of monasticism, fiery zeal for the defence of orthodox doctrine – these were the distinguishing marks of Epiphanius. They were accompanied by a lack of moderation, calmness, prudence and knowledge of men and affairs which occasioned many difficulties for him towards the end of his life. He had always strongly opposed Origen's doctrines and in 392 or 394 he visited Jerusalem, a centre of Origen's supporters and admirers, amongst whom was John II, bishop of Jerusalem. (Jerome, in Bethlehem, and Rufinus were admirers of Origen also.) Epiphanius delivered an address strongly condemning

Origen, in John's presence, before a great assembly in the Church of the Holy Sepulchre. John refused to condemn Origen and Epiphanius broke off communion with him. Rufinus took John's side and Jerome took the side of his friend'papa Epiphanius pentaglottos'. Epiphanius then ordained Paulinian (St. Jerome's brother) in John's diocese, and against John's will. Theophilus of Alexandria finally reconciled them.

Theophilus held Origenistic views but declared himself anti-Origenist about 399 and expelled Egyptian Origenist monks from the Nitrian desert. Some of them fled for refuge to John Chrysostom to Constantinople, whom Theophilus declared suspect (of Origenism) and Epiphanius was called upon as an ally against Chrysostom. (There was always acute rivalry between Alexandria and Constantinople.) Epiphanius, 402, at a synod in Cyprus condemned Origen and his writings, and then set out for Constantinople to conduct the war against heresy there personally. He failed to see through the duplicity of Theophilus for some time, but finally desisted from his campaign against Chrysostom, and without waiting for the Synod of the Oak (where Chrysostom was deposed) he left for Cyprus and died at sea, 12 May 403.

Writings. Practically all are political and concerned with the refutation of heresy.

(1) *Anchoratus* (ankurotos) the firmly-anchored man. In 374 at the request of friends in Pamphylia he wrote this book, expounding in it the doctrine of the Trinity, especially of the Holy Ghost. Its purpose is to provide safe anchorage for those cast about on the waves of Arian and semi-Arian controversies. It contains many digressions. Two *Creeds* at the end of it are important. They were addressed to the community at Syedra, to be used at baptism. Caspari has shown that the second and longer one was now composed by Epiphanius himself, while the other is a baptismal creed of earlier origin and was introduced into Constantia not long before Epiphanius's election. Accepted (with a few modifications) by the Council of Constantinople (381), it became the Profession of Faith for the whole Church and the baptismal creed of the East (see Kelly o.c.).

(2) *Panarion* (against eighty heresies) (374-377) the 'medicine chest' i.e. antidote for those bitten by the serpent of heresy and protection for those of sound faith. He reckons amongst heresies the Greek philosophical schools and religious sects of the Jews – twenty are B.C. He is greatly indebted to St.

110

Irenaeus and St. Justin and St. Hippolytus. The work is important as a source-book. His sources for the latter heresies are rich historical material though he lacked critical acumen.

(3) *Weights and measures* – composed at Constantinople, 392 – treats of the canon and versions of the Old Testament and Pt. 2 describes the biblical weights and measures; Pt. 3 of the geography of Palestine. It is extant in a Syriac version.

(4) *The Twelve Precious Stones* – in the breast-plate of the high priest, dedicated to Diodorus of Tarsus is extant in Latin.

DIODORE OF TARSUS

Diodore of Tarsus (c. 395) was born of noble parentage, an illustrious Antioch family, was highly gifted and industrious and received the best education his age could give in his native schools and at Athens. He shared in the government of a monastic community near Antioch for many decades. Julian the Apostate paid the highest tribute to his merits in a letter published later (545-551) by Facundus of Hermiane – that Diodore 'had equipped his malevolent tongue against the ancient gods with the wisdom of Athens herself'. Circumstances made Diodore's writings apologetic and polemical in character. In Antioch the conflict between Catholic and Arian was very bitter, and especially under the Arian emperors Constantius (337-361) and Valens (364-378). Julian tried to restore paganism, and as his winter quarters were at Antioch, his influence was powerful there. Diodore was a close friend of Flavian (elected in 381 as successor to Meletius, the bishop of Antioch) who guarded the interests of the faith in Antioch. 'Flavian and Diodorus rose like two great rocks in the ocean on the firm sides of which the towering waves broke in vain... Diodorus wise and strong was like a broad clear river, the waters of which slaked the thirst of his own people but swept away the blasphemies of his enemies'. (Theodoret). He had to fly from Antioch in 372. He met Basil. He was made bishop of Tarsus (378) and he took part in the Council of Constantinople (381).

Writings. Only fragments remain. He was a very copious writer. (1) *Commentaries* on the whole Bible, adopting the historico-grammatical method and opposing firmly the mystico-allegorical interpretation of the Alexandrines. (2) *'On the*

111

difference between theory and allegory' – a work of great importance in the study of hermeneutical principles. (3) *Apologetic and Dogmatic works*, known only by their titles. *Contra Astronomos astrologos, et Fatum* – eight books; *Contra Manichaeos* – twenty-five books.

Doctrine. Diodore was esteemed by contemporaries as a pillar of orthodoxy – after his death he was accused of heresy. His writings contained in germ the errors that his disciple Theodore was to develop into Nestorianism. In seeking to defend Christ's divinity against the Arians and His humanity against the Apollinarists he weakened the union of the divine and human so that it became a mere indwelling of the Logos in a man. In 483 Cyril of Alexandria wrote three books against Theodore of Mopsuestia and Diodore accusing them as originators of Nestorianism.

THEODORE OF MOPSUESTIA

Theodore of Mopsuestia (c. 350-428) was born at Antioch of noble family and studied under the famous sophist Libanius. He intended becoming a lawyer but, at the entreaty of his friend John Chrysostom, he embraced the monastic life and retired to the monastery of Diodore where he led an ascetic life and studied Sacred Scripture. He tired of the monastic life, but an eloquent letter of Chrysostom brought about a change of heart, and he returned to the monastery. Flavian of Antioch ordained him priest (383) and in 392 he was appointed bishop of Mopsuestia in Cilicia where he became an important figure in the ecclesiastical life of the East. He remained a staunch friend of the exiled St. John Chrysostom. During his episcopate, as before it, he assailed heresy vigorously. He died in 328.

Theodore was a man of extensive knowledge and learning, a student of the Antioch grammatico-literal school, and a determined opponent of Alexandrine allegory and Alexandrine Christological teaching. His extreme reaction against the former led him to an almost entirely spiritual interpretation of the Bible. He admitted only four Psalms as Messianic (2,3, 44, 109) and declared the Canticle of Canticles to be a mere love poem. Many of his poems show him to have been really a 'Nestorius before Nestorius'. He taught two persons in Christ and the fifth General Council condemned him and his writings and anathematised many individual Christological theses (553). As a result many of his works have been lost to us. He was accused of being a Pelagian also. His doctrine is substantially Pelagian for he denies original sin. His catecheses recently discovered him shown as a zealous and good shepherd and excellent homilist.

Works. (1) *Exegetical.* Commentaries on Genesis, Psalms, the minor Prophets, Sts. John, Matthew and Luke; ten minor epistles of St. Paul. Also Samuel, Job, Ecclesiastes; Major Prophets (lost). (2) *Dogmatic Works* against Arians, Apollinarists, Monophysitism. *Ad Patrophilum* (Against Pneumatomachi) is extant. (3) *Catecheses* – instructions for catechumens on the mysteries of the faith (Creed, Lord's Prayers, Baptism, Confirmation and Eucharist).

ST. JOHN CHRYSOSTOM

St. John Chrysostom, Doctor of the Church, (344-407). Only a brief outline of his life and activities is possible here. John, surnamed Golden-mouthed, was born in 344 or 347 in Antioch of Christian parents – Secundus and Anthusa – and brought up in surroundings of splendour and affluence. One of his teachers was the famous rhetorician Libanius, under whom he had as fellow students, Theodore, and one Basil (not Magnus). John gave up the promise of a brilliant career for prayer and study, studied Christian doctrine under Meletius of Antioch and was baptized in 369. Diodorus also taught him. He intended to pursue the monastic life, but his widowed mother begged him not to leave her. He and Basil were selected for the episcopate c. 373; Basil accepted apparently on John's promise that he would accept also. But John ran away and his six books on the Priesthood were written to justify his conduct to his friend whom he had offended by his action. After his mother's death he retired to a mountain district near Antioch and spent four years there and two years in a cave in ascetic practices and in study. He was forced by ill-health to return to Antioch. Meletius (381) ordained him deacon and Flavian priest (386). Flavian gave him the duty of preaching in the chief church of the city, and here he preached his famous sermons for almost twelve years, and achieved renown throughout the whole East.

Constantinople. When Nectarius died in 397, Chrysostom, at the suggestion of the emperor Arcadius, was chosen as his successor as patriarch, and was taken by stealth and violence

113

from Antioch to his see. Theophilus of Alexandria objected, but was himself compelled to consecrate John. The latter began a thorough reform of his church and aroused great opposition. The weak and narrow-minded emperor was completely in the hands of the eunuch Eutropius who was unprincipled, avaricious and ambitious. Chrysostom fearlessly opposed Eutropius. The story of Eutropius's fall from grace and power, his taking refuge in Chrysostom's church though he had disputed with John the right of sanctuary and Chrysostom's celebrated sermon on the event ('Vanity of Vanities') are well known.

Eudoxia, the empress, succeeded to the power which Eutropius lost and she soon became Chrysostom's bitter enemy. In 400 he left his see for some months to compose certain difficulties at the request of Ephesus and a party was formed against him. Theophilus watched for an opportunity to bring about his downfall. The Egyptian monks were divided into followers and opponents of Origen. Theophilus expelled the Origenists, who fled to Constantinople for refuge. Chrysostom received them, but with reserve, pending an explanation from their bishop. Theophilus was summoned to Constantinople by the emperor to give an account to a Synod presided over by Chrysostom. Chrysostom declined to try him. Theophilus arrived with a great retinue (25) of Egyptian bishops and turned the tables on his judge. We have seen the Epiphanius incident already.

Chrysostom delivered a homily on the luxury of women and their inordinate love of ornament. It was taken to be an attack on Eudoxia who now urged Theophilus to come and hold a synod and depose Chrysostom. Thirty-six bishops met near Chalcedon (The Oak) in August 403 and summoned Chrysostom on thirty frivolous charges – the affair of the monks was ignored. Chrysostom held a synod of forty bishops but agreed to go to the other gathering if Theophilus and three other enemies left it. The *Synod of the Oak* then condemned him for contumacy, deposed him, and referred to the emperor a charge of treason (calling the empress a Jezabel, Palladius). The emperor condemned him to banishment. Intense feeling was aroused. An earthquake shook Constantinople and Eudoxia was so alarmed that she recalled him, and her messengers overtook him at Prenetum (Bithynia). His return was a triumphal progress – (cf. Athanasius and Alexandria).

The truce did not last long. Two months later (403) Eudoxia caused a silver statue of herself to be erected just outside the

114

church and the noise and celebrations, interrupted the cere-monies there. Chrysostom requested the city prefect to put an end to the disturbance. This was construed by Eudoxia as an insult and she determined to be rid of him. Socrates and Sozomen relate that Chrysostom answered her violence with violent language. Theophilus, through his envoys, caused certain canons of Antioch of 341 to be invoked against him (that a bishop deposed by one synod must be reinstated by a larger synod – violators of this to be permanently dispossessed of their see). The canons were not universally admitted. The emperor ordered Chrysostom to cease performing ecclesiastical functions. He refused. On Holy Saturday, 404, he went to his church to baptize catechumens and at night-fall soldiers came and drove the faithful from the church. A few days after Pentecost, to avoid a popular rising, Chrysostom left secretly. He learned at Nicaea that he was to go to Cucusus (Lesser Armenia) 'the most abandoned spot in the world'. Arsacius first, then Atticus, succeeded in Constantinople, but the Johannites refused to recognise them. Eudoxia died a few months afterwards. The West broke off communion with Atticus. From Cucusus Chrysostom maintained contact with his flock, and with Antioch, and he was ordered to go to Pityus, on the eastern extremity of the Black Sea. Towards the end of June 407, he set out for Pityus, and at Comana in Pontus he died, worn out by the hardships of the journey – 14 September. The schism in Constantinople was finally ended when the earthly remains of the saint were brought back to the city, and interred in the Church of the Apostles. Theo-dosius II, son of Eudoxia, met the funeral train, and 'begged the he would intercede with God for his parents who had sinned through ignorance' (Theodoret).

Works. No other Greek Father has left so extensive a literary legacy.

(1) **Exegetical Homilies.** (a) *In Genesin (Genesis)* h. 67 (386-88); (b) *In Psalmos* h. 58 (397); (c) *In Isaiam*; (d) *In Matthaeum* h. 90 (386-87); (e) *In Joannem* h. 88 (389); (f) *In epistolas S. Pauli, (The Letters of St. Paul)* – these are his most famous homilies and were delivered in great part in Antioch. They breathe throughout his great personal love of St. Paul. *Homilies on Ep. ad Romanos* are the most outstanding.

(2) **Discourses.** (a) *De Statuis* 21 (387). The citizens of Antioch had protested against taxation by overturning the emperor's statues. While Flavian went to intercede with the

emperor, Chrysostom delivered these – Lent 387. (b) *In Eutropium* (399); (c) *On St. Paul* – seven panegyrics (Antioch); (d) *De incomprehensibili* – twelve homilies against the Anomoeans (386); (e) *Adv. Judaeos*, h. 8 (386), et. etc.

(3) **Moral and Ascetic Treatises.** Numerous. (a) *De inani gloria et de liberis educandis* (393) – a valuable work on education; (b) *De Sacerdotio* – six books (381-85) in the form of a dialogue between John and Basil. In its style, elegance, matter it ranks highest amongst his works. – No author of antiquity speaks in so sublime a manner of the dignity and function of a priest. St. Gregory of Nazianzus's *De Fuga* was a source. No writing of Chrysostom has been so frequently translated and printed and none is so famous. His book *On Pride and the Education of Children* is the first handbook on Christian education; in this sphere the saint holds first place easily.

(4) **Letters.** 238 extant from the time of his exile (404-407). Chief amongst them are seventeen *Ad Olympiam,* widow. They are exceptionally cordial and frank. 'In many... there shines a soul so magnanimous as to be no longer accessible to external sorrow or wrong, so closely united with God as to seem long since vanished from life on earth'. (Bardenhewer).

Character and **Greatness.** Ordained priest after the Arian controversies were over and in his decline before the next great Christological heresies were to arise in the East, living during a truce in the 'wars of the Lord', Chrysostom was denied by opportunity a place among the architects of dogma. Less than a century after his death he was called 'Golden-mouthed' by the Orient in tribute to his chief claim to greatness. 'He is not only the mightiest orator of Greek Christianity; Demosthenes alone of orators who spoke in Greek has had a wider posthumous audience. His thought and pictures and very words were the texture for countless sermons in the centuries following his own. His structureless homiletic method and gorgeous rhetorical ornaments fell out of fashion at last, but not his thought, for Chrysostom by preference treated of moral themes in the pulpit, which are in fashion in every age'. (Campbell). The most successful exemplar of the *Antiochene method*, he combined depth and breadth and delicacy, even allegory, in a surpassing fashion. He became a mighty authority in East and West on the *content of the faith* – first invoked by the Latins though bishop of Constantinople, honoured in Alexandria though he had been priest of hostile Antioch. Though he contributed nothing to the development of a special point in

116

dogma 'he was in the thick of the controversies which arose after his death, the ally desired by all protagonists in the struggle for orthodox sanction' (Campbell). What progress was made in *education* in his time is associated with him (see comparison with St. Augustine, P.157).

'Orator, exegete, essayist, educationalist, witness to and confessor of the Faith, St. John Chrysostom is the best known and the best loved of the Greek Fathers. More of him has survived, he has been translated more frequently and more widely than any other Father of the Orient. Origen alone influenced the after-world more deeply not even Origen influenced it more tangibly... The Antiochenes called him 'Great Teacher of the Earth' and Pope Celestine repeated the title. Within half a century of his death he was acknowledged a doctor of the Church. Pope and patriarch and council appealed regularly to his authoritative witness. From the tenth century he was, along with St. Basil and St. Gregory of Nazianzus, one of the three Hierarchs of the Greek Church. He came to be considered its greatest saint, extracts from whom were read to the people on feast-days... In the education of Byzantine youth he had a place alongside Homer and Isocrates. To such authority he grew in the East, as East and West fell away, breaking at times even in his Greek original the indifference of that long separation, returning to the West among the first of the Greek fathers in the Renaissance days to meet the survivals of his Latinised self (Campbell). 'Animo mitis et dulcis... in vindicandis Ecclesiae iuribus erat fortissimus, in abusibus castigandis intrepidus, in labore pastorali indefessus. Propter doctrinam suam eucharisticam 'Doctor eucharistiae' vocatur'. Gentle and charming in disposition... he was most valiant in defence of the Church's rights, fearless in the correction of abuses, tireless in pastoral labours; his theology of the Eucharist has earned for him the title 'Doctor of the Eucharist', (Steidle).

Cardinal Newman (*Historical Sketches, II*, 234, 237) wrote: 'His unrivalled charm... lies in his singleness of purpose, his fixed grasp of his aim, his noble earnestness. A bright, cheerful, gentle soul; a sensitive heart, a temperament open to emotion and impulse; and all this elevated, refined, transformed by the touch of heaven. He was indeed a man to make both friends and enemies, to inspire affection and kindle resentment; but his friends loved him with a love that was 'stronger' than 'death' and his enemies hated him with a hatred that was more

117

'burning' than 'hell', and it was well to be so hated, if he was so beloved'.

(See *Selections from St. John Chrysostom*. The Greek Text edited, with Introduction and Commentary. By (Cardinal) J. F. D'Alton London, 1940. 'St. John Chrysostom in Exile', *Ir. Ecc. Record*, September 1935), by the same author.

ST. CYRIL OF ALEXANDRIA

St. Cyril of Alexandria (?-444), Doctor of the Church, succeeded his uncle Theophilus in Alexandria in 412, and practically nothing is known of his life until then. It is stated that he spent some time under the direction of the monks. His works show him to have been educated in Alexandria. In 403 he accompanied his uncle to the Synod of the Oak and like Theophilus was all his life opposed to St. Chrysostom and his memory. This was mainly due to the traditional hositility between Alexandria (which claimed to be the Second See of the Church) and Constantinople (Nova Roma). His early years as patriarch were marked by severe, even violent measures against the Novatians and Jews. Socrates alleges great harshness and want of feeling on his part. Cyrils' dissensions with Orestes, city prefect, were many, and enemies of Cyril went so far as even to throw on him some of the responsibility for the murder of Hypatia, a female philosopher and close friend of Orestes. She was brutally done to death (March 415) by some Christians – she was identified with the effort (cf. Julian's) to restore the pagan way of life. It was only after long resistance (417) Cyril allowed Chrysostom's name to be replaced in the diptychs of the Alexandrian church. He is in the centre of all the dogmatic problems and discussions. 'Amid perils and trials his spirit and character shine as in noonday splendour and exhibit in him an instrument specially chosen by God'. (Bardenhewer).

From 428 the controversy with Nestorius and Antioch theologians began, and it was carried on with a spirit and acrimony and bitterness for which not only zeal for orthodoxy was responsible but also the opposition of Antioch and Alexandria as schools, and private and political rivalries and enmities between Constantinople and Alexandria. Nestorius became bishop of Constantinople in 428, and began to teach (cf. Diodore's and Theodore's teaching) that the Blessed Virgin could not be called *Theotokos, deipara,* God-bearing

118

Mother of God, and said it was error to speak of God as in swaddling clothes, being crucified. Cyril, 429, replied to this in a Festal Letter, and an Encyclical Letter to the monks of Egypt. Pope Celestine was appealed to by both and in 430 a synod held at Rome, condemned Nestorius as heretical and deposed of him unless he retracted his teaching. Cyril was deputed to convey the decision and to excommunicate him in case of contumacy. Cyril added a profession of faith approved in Alexandria in 430 and twelve 'Anathemas' describing the errors Nestorius was to reject. Nestorius replied with twelve counter-anathemas and this completed the rupture.

Theodosius yielded to the pleas of Nestorius and convoked (19 Nov. 430) a council at Ephesus for Pentecost 431. The Pope delegated Cyril to act for him. Nestorius was condemned. Cyril's profession of faith and anathemas were confirmed but not defined and the twelve anathemas were lost sight of for a century afterwards. Cyril presided and discharged a difficult mission with energy and prudence. The Antiochene bishops, under John's leaderschip, had Theodosius II so firmly on their side that Cyril and Memnon (Ephesus) were imprisoned for some months. Not until 433 was a reconciliation effected and that year Cyril signed a profession of faith (very probably drawn up by Theodoret of Cyrus, the most learned of the Antiochenes) that was capable of an orthodox interpretation and acknowledged an 'inconfusa unio utriusque naturae' (union of natures without mingling) in Christ, the divine maternity of Mary. Ecclesiasistal unity was formally restored but Cyril had to devote the remainder of his life to dealing with it.

St Cyril is reckoned as one of the outstanding Fathers and theologians of the Church. He was a great public man raised up by God to defend Christological doctrine in face of serious opposition, doctrinal, political, personal. Opponents of the Church and Cyril point to indications of absence of saintly meekness. Cyril exerted a wider influence on ecclesiastical doctrine than any Greek Father except Athanasius, and apart from St. Augustine there is not a Father whose works have been adopted so extensively by the ecumenical councils as a standard expression of faith. He has been called 'sigillum Patrum'. He defended and expounded the Trinitarian doctrine of the Greek Fathers especially on the Holy Ghost, but his chief glory lies in his courageous and brilliant defence and exposition of the union of the divine and human nature in one divine Person in Christ against Antioch rationalism. It has

119

been alleged that his Christological formulae prepared the way for Monophysitism – containing the germs of heresy objectively. Dioscurus, his successor and ardent disciple, was condemned at Chalcedon, 451, for Monophysitism. Indeed the ancient and illustrious church of Alexandria perished as a result of this heresy. Cyril's Christology, and a surprising statement (after his reconciliation with the Antiochenes): before the union there were two natures *(physeis)* and after it but one *(physis)* are discussed in Bardenhewer, o.c., 77. He means and teaches the union of the Logos with a perfect human nature, composed of a body and a rational soul — this nature however, does not subsist independently in itself but in the Logos. 'We say that two natures, *physeis*, are united but after the union there is no longer a division into two (natures); we believe in one nature of the Son, because He is one, though become man and flesh'. He uses the words *henosis physica, (union of natures), henosis kath hypostasin, (substantial unity)*. He teaches the Word became man, did not assume man – He united Himself with our human nature in a substantial or personal union; He is after the Incarnation what He was before – He remained what He was. He assumed our human nature to the unity of His own being and is now both God and man. Cyril uses as if equivalent the terms *hypostasis* and *physis*. So the phrase *mia physis tou theou logou sesarkomene, (One incarnate nature of God the Word)*, caused him to be accused of a teaching a commingling of two natures – he insists always, however, on a union without commingling or confusion (synchysis)... As a consequence of the union of the two natures we can say God suffered – the Logos suffered and died – God was born and Mary is the Mother of God. Hence *Theotokos, (Godbearing)* instead of Nestorian *Christotokos, (Mother of Christ)* or *anthropotokos, (Mother of a man)*. Cyril said 'a correct, sufficient, and irreproachable profession of faith is found in the assertion of the divine maternity of the Blessed Virgin'. *(Hom. 15 de Incarn. Dei)*.

Works.

(1) **Apology against Julian.** a. 433., dedicated to Theodosius II. Julian's three books *Against the Gallilians* (362-63) must have been still popular. Ten of Cyril's thirty books survive (1-10) – and some fragments. Cyril's work is our chief source for Julian's lost work – he states Julian's charges and then answers them.

(2) **Exegetical.** (a) *De adoratione et cultu in spiritu et veritate,*

120

seventeen books (429) – allegory and the Old Testament. (b) *Glaphyra* (ante 429) – elegant comments on select Pentateuch passages. (c) Commentaries on Isaias, minor Prophets, Psalms, Samuel, Kings, Proverbs, etc. (d) Comm. on St. John. (e) Comm. (fragments) on St. Matthew, Romans, Corinthians and Hebrews. (f) St. Luke – sixteen homilies.

(3) **Dogmatico-Polemical.** The polemical note is predominant in all his dogmatic writings. (a) *Thesaurus de sancta et consubstantiali trinitate* in thirty-five theses or chapters refuting errors and stating doctrine. (b) *De Sancta et consubstantiali trinitate* – seven dialogues: Against Arians (a. 425). (c) *In sanctum symbolum* (Nicene). (d) *Adversus Nestorii blasphemias contradictionum libri* 5 – solid argument and cutting sarcasm. (e) *De recta fide ad Augustum et Dominas*, two books on the same problem. (f) *Apologeticus ad imperatorem* (431). (g) *Anathematisms* 12 (430). In defence of these he wrote three commentaries (i) Explanation, (ii) Explanation, (iii) Letter to Euoptius against Theodoret's attack on the twelve Anathematisms. Theodoret stated the Antiochene teaching and accused Cyril of Apollinarism and Monophysitism. (h) Treatises on the Incarnation, Hypostatic Union, Theotokos. (i) *Contra Synusiastas* (extreme Apollinarists).

Letters. Festal Letters (29). Eighty-eight besides (17 to Cyril), three of which are called ecumenical (commended at Ephesus, Chalcedon and Constantinople Councils), numbers 4, 17, 39. On Christology, *Sermons* – a few extant.

THEODORET OF CYRUS

Theodoret of Cyrus (c. 386-458), born at Antioch and educated there under Chrysostom and Theodore of Mopsuestia, with Nestorius as fellow-pupil, became bishop of Cyrus, near Antioch. He displayed tireless zeal in the administration of his diocese and in restoring unity of faith there. He suspected Cyril's doctrine of Apollinarism and opposed his anathemas. He maintained this opposition even after Ephesus, and refused to agree to the terms of reconciliation between Cyril and the bishops of the East in 433. The Union-Creed Cyril then accepted was Theodoret's, who saw in Cyril's act a withdrawal of the error contained in his anathemas. It was only in 435 that Theodoret accepted the bishop's terms after John of Antioch had renounced his demand for a formal recognition of the condemnation of Nestorius, Eutyches of Constantinople asserted that there was in Christ only one nature, *physis*, (not in Cyril's sense of one person) in the sense of a compound nature. Dioscorus, patriarch of Alexandria, sympathised with this error opposed to Nestorianism, and at the Robber-Synod of Ephesus (449) deposed Theodoret. The Emperor Marcian recalled him in 450 and Pope Leo reinstated him. He assited at the Council of Chalcedon (451), and after concurring in the anathema against Nestorius was completely rehabilitated, and lived at peace in the Church until his death in 458.

Writings

(1) **Apologetic Works.** He composed the last and the most perfect of the early Graeco-Christian apologies, known as *Graecarum affectionum Curatio.* He refutes the heathen objection that the Apostles were unlettered and (Bks. 2-12) compares the heathen and Christian answers to the important questions in philosophy and theology – origin of the world, our destiny, etc. All the preceding apologies are made use of, especially the *Stromata* and Eusebius's *Evangelical Preparation* (427).

(2) **Dogmatico-Polemical**. (430). *Pentalogium* (Against Cyil); *On the holy and vivifying Trinity; On the Incarnation of the Lord; The Beggar or the Polymorph* (447) against Monophysitism. The Monophysites, he says, have collected miscellaneous folly beggarwise from Cerdo, Marcion, Arius etc.

(3) **Exegetical.** Treatises on the Pentateuch, Josue, Judges, Ruth, Kings, Paralipomenon – commentaries on Psalms, Canticle of Canticles, all the prophets, on the Epistles of St. Paul. He 'is held to be the greatest exegete of Graeco-Christian antiquity. His commentaries are both copious and excellent in contents, also incomparable models of exegetical style, by reason of their compactness, brevity, and transparent lucidity of diction'. He follows the Antiochene principles of exegesis He does not pretend to originality, yet he is no mere compiler. 'It may be said that with Theodoret the golden age of the Antiochene school closes; it fell to him to hand over to posterity its highest achievements, and right nobly did he perform his task' (Bardenhewer).

Historical. His *Church History* (450) is very valuable and, taking up where Eusebius leaves off, he treats of the Church from the Arian to the Nestorian troubles (323-428). *History of the Monks* (444) – life of the celebrated ascetics of the East.

122

Compendium of Heretical Tables (after 451) – account of heresies.

(5) **Homilies and Letters.** Most of the former have perished. The latter 'not to speak of their value for the history of dogma and the history of the Church – have always been prized for the polish and grace of their style, their felicitous diction, and the unpretentious learning that they display'. Forty-eight letters, first made known by Sakkelion (1885).

MINOR WRITERS: FIFTH CENTURY

(a) **Macarius Magnes'** Apologist (410).

(b) **Church Historians,** About 430, *Philippus Sidetes* (Pamphylia) published a 'Christian History' – he published also a reply to Julian's three books *Against the Galileans. Hesychius* (Jerusalem), *Timotheus of Berytus, Sabinus of Thrace* – historians. Little is known of most of their work.

(1) **Socrates** of Constantinople wrote seven books of Church History to continue the narrative of Eusebius from the abdication of Diocletian (305) to 439. (2) **Sozomen** of Constantinople – Church History – nine books from 324-425, and a compendium of ecclesiastical history up to A.D. 323.

(c) **Exegetes.** A monk *Adrian* (400-450) wrote an Introduction to the Sacred Scriptures *(eisagoge, 'introduction')* – the term appears here for the first time. *St. Isidore* of Pelusium. *Hesychius* of Jerusalem (433).

(d) **Ascetic Writers.** Palladius (363-425) bishop in Asia Minor, about 420 compiled a number of monastic biographies – *Historia Lausiaca* – from the name of Lausus, an official. Palladius is Chrysostom's biographer and not the bishop of Hellenopolis in Bithynia. The history is a reliable and valuable account of early monastic life. St. Nilus is a prominent ascetic writer, also Marcus Eremita, Arsenius (Egypt).

(e) **Poets.** *Claudianus* and *Cyrus*. Under Claudian's name are seven Greek epigrams, two adressed to Our Lord, and two fragments of a Greek *Gigantomachia*. It is believed that Claudian is the celebrated Latin poet Claudian (c. 408) under whose name we have some brief Latin Christian poems *(Carmen Paschale, 'Easter Hymn,' Laus Christi,' 'The Praise of Christ', Miracula, 'Wonders')*.

GOLDEN AGE. SECOND SECTION: SYRIAC WRITERS

The most ancient documents of Syriac authorship we know of are the *Diatessaron, Melito*'s discourse, works (Gnostic) of Bardesanes, Acts of Thomas and the Teaching of Addaeus. From the second century the theological school of Edessa was a seminary for the Persian clergy and the centre of academic and literary activity in Syria. Ephraem (4th century) is one of its best representatives. The school was related closely to that of Antioch and devoted to the literal interpretation of Scripture. The East-Syrian school is Oriental as compared with the West-Syrian. It is more poetical, mystical and contemplative, averse to change or evolution, or speculative thought. The Church of Syria was deeply and irreparably injured by the Christological heresies, and Edessa was the last prop of Nestorianism in the Empire. Zeno closed it in 489 for this reason, but from its ruins rose the Nestorian school of Nisibis in Persia. Monophysitism had strong supporters there, too, and Justinian's efforts to suppress it were rendered futile by the activity of Jacob Baradaeus (Bishop of Edessa from 541) – hence the name Jacobites for Syrian Monophysites. Syriac literature depends largely on Greek literature, many Greek Fathers having been translated into Syriac.

APHRAATES

Aphraates (367), Jacob Aphraates, 'the Persian sage', was a monk and became a bishop of Mar Mathaeus (St. Matthew), east of Mosul, and an important figure in the Mesopotamian hierarchy. In 1869 W. Wright discovered the Syriac original text of twenty-three homilies written A.D. 336, 343, 345. His style though diffuse is clear and simple, and his diction pure and uncontaminated by foreign words – he did not know the Greek works. His writings have a very great philological value and are of fundamental importance for Syriac syntax. His Christological ideas are those of Nicene Fathers. He defended the unity of the Church against the Gnostics, and treated of Baptism, the Eucharist and Penance rather fully.

124

ST. EPHRAEM

St. Ephraem, Deacon, Doctor of the Church (306-373), is the most important writer of the Syrian patristic age, and reckoned as one of the greatest of the Syrian Fathers and poets. He is styled 'Lyre of the Holy Spirit', and his praises were sung by the whole East. He was born at Nisibis about 306 of Christian parents, became a hermit, and was made headmaster of the school of Nisibis. The city was besieged by Sapor II in 338, 346, and 350 and passed into his hands in 363. Ephraem and most the Christians went to the Roman territory and lived at Edessa where most of his writings were composed. He seems to have resumed his hermit's life near the city. He travelled to Caesarea (Cappad) to see Basil in 370 and is said to have received deaconship from him. He died in 373.

Writings. He left an extraordinary number of works, possibly commentaries on the entire Scriptures, and he treated in metrical works numerous points of doctrine and discipline. The Syrians called him 'eloquent mouth', 'doctor of the world', 'pillar of the Church', and several of his hymns were adopted in the Syrian liturgies. At an early date his works were translated into Greek, Armenian, Coptic, Arabic, Ethiopian.

Exegetical. His commentaries are in prose and in the Antiochene tradition, excellent in their exposition. There are extant commentaries (Syriac) on Genesis and Exodus and Armenian versions of treatises on Tatian's *Diatessaron*, Acts of the Apostles, Epistles of St. Paul (including three to Corinthians and excluding one to Philemon).

Dogmatic-Polemical. Practically all his treatises are polemical – against Bardesanes, Marcion, etc.

Homiletic etc. These are in metre and the homilies usually run into equi-syllabic lines (seven-syllable lines – the Ephraemic metre). His moralising discourses, monitory or penitential, form the greater part of his works. There are four poems against Julian the Apostate. His poems are doctrinal, moral, polemical, liturgical, poems of Nisibis etc. and 'his harp resounds to the praises of Mary more frequently than that of any other poet or orator of Christian antiquity. He loves to sing of her stainless virginity, her truly divine maternity, her freedom from sin' (Bardenhewer).

THIRD SECTION: LATIN WRITERS

General conspectus. Though the Trinitarian and Christological heresies affected the Western Church, the peculiar characteristics of the West led to a consideration of the practical duty of man to God rather than speculation on the idea of God. There was, in this period, only one notable doctrinal controversy in the West – on the necessity of God's co-operation with man's efforts to attain his end. It is ecclesiastical anthropology that is developed in opposition to Pelagianism and Semipelagianism. The Novatian and Donatist schisms occasioned discussion of the nature of the Church and the efficacy of the sacraments. St. Hilary of Poitiers devoted his literary talents to the refutation of Arianism and drew copiously on Eastern sources. He was a channel through which Western thought was enriched by the speculation of the Eastern Church. He, St. Jerome and Rufinus (interested in biblico-historical questions), Marius Mercator and John Cassian were 'Grecising Westerns' mediators between Greek and Latin theology. Specifically Western are Ambrose, Augustine, Leo the Great. Ambrose is the first to attempt a complete exposition of Christian morals teaching as distinct from Christian faith (after the manner of Cicero's *De officiis*), but in exegesis he borrows from Origen and Hippolytus and in dogma from Basil whom he resembled in many ways. In Augustine the sovereignty of the Greek Fathers in speculative thought passed to the West and his mighty intellect, acute, profound, vast, ranged through the manifold problems of theology and anthropology with ease. 'He breathed a new life into nearly all branches of ecclesiastical science, laboured at them with creative vigour, and set before them new tasks and aims'; and for a thousand years after his time the Greek Fathers were eclipsed in the West, influencing that West only anonymously, as an element unrecognised in an accepted common tradition. Leo the Great, Doctor, enjoyed a pre-eminence of intellect in the Monophysite conflict 'quite worthy of the mighty energy with which he governed and directed the ecclesiastical' world of the time.

A theological school appears in the newly-founded monasteries on the Isle of Lerins, and near Marseilles. (John Cassian, and Vincent of Lerins).

126

Theological literature becomes more aggressive than defensive in its apologetic. Firmicius Maternus attacks pagan mysteries, Ambrose and Prudentius heathenism in Roman life, Augustine and Orosius the deities. Hilary, Lucifer of Calaris, Ambrose, Augustine assailed Arianism; John Cassian and Marius Mercator Nestorianism; Leo Monophysitism; Pacian and Ambrose vindicated the power of the keys against Novatianism; Optatus of Mileve and Augustine fought Donatism. Pelagius presented the West with its greatest theological difficulty and was refuted by Augustine, Jerome, Orosius, Marius Mercator. **Biblical Theology** finds its best scholar in Jerome who gave the West its finest translation of the Bible and admirable works on Biblical Introduction and Archaeology. His commentaries fall below our expectation, are hurried, and suffer from lack of clear hermeneutic principle. Hilary, Ambros, Augustine affect allegory in their exegesis. In **Historical Theology** little was done save in translating from the Greek (Jerome and Rufinus). Sulpicius Severus, Orosius, Augustine, Jerome, Rufinus and Paulinus did some original work also. **Practical Theology**, Ambrose, Jerome, Augustine. After these as orators come Leo the Great, Peter Chrysologus and Maximus of Turin. **Poetry.** Latins were more productive in poetry than the Greeks. Didactic poems (cf. Commodian) were written by Prudentius, Paulinus of Nola, Augustine, Prosper of Aquitaine, Orientius and others. A number attempted epic poetry – Proba (biblical history), Cyprian of Gaul, etc. Pope Damasus, Prudentius, Paulinus of Nola composed panegyrical poems on Christ and the saints. This poetry is the same as the Roman epic except for subject matter, but the lyric poetry of Latin Christianity is a new species, the hymn.

FIRMICIUS MATERNUS

Firmicius Maternus (post 360) is a Sicilian rhetorician of whose life we know little. Probably he is the author of a work on astrology, *Mathesis* (334-337), and after his conversion he wrote *De Errore profanarum religionum* (343-350), an apology directed to Constantine and Constans. It is a direct attack on the 'mysteries' on which paganism was making its last stand, on the superstition and immorality of them. There is a certain violence and fanaticism in the attack but 'the heathenism of the fourth century was never described in a more true and

127

reliable manner than in this book'. The long passage (c. 18) on the Blessed Eucharist is of dogmatic importance.

ST. HILARY OF POITIERS

St. Hilary of Poitiers, Doctor of the Church, was born at Poitiers about 315 of a noble pagan family and baptized in 345 when he was already married and had a daughter (Abra). It was a very troubled period for the Church and the Arian discords had made their way as far as Gaul. Jerome in 399 wrote on the results of the double synod of Seleucia – Rimini (359), *'Ingemuit totus orbis et Arianum se esse miratus est'* (*'The whole world groaned and was thunderstruck at finding itself Arian')*. The people and clergy of Poitiers unanimously chose Hilary for their bishop (before 355) and he was from that moment the leading figure in the struggle in the West against Arianism. He was the foremost champion of orthodoxy at the Synod of Paris (355) in which the Gallic bishops dissociated themselves from the Arians Ursacius and Valens, and Saturninus of Arles. The latter called a synod at Beziers, to which Hilary was summoned by Constantius (356) and for refusal to submit to the emperor's religious policy he was banished to Phrygia (356).

Exile lasted for four years during which he remained comparatively free and active and made himself very familiar with the Greek Fathers, especially their works on the Trinity. This was to be of great service to him later. The Arians caused him to be sent home to Gaul as 'a disturber of the peace of the East' (360). On his return he set about healing the wounds inflicted by Arianism on his diocese and on Gaul. Many bishops had accepted the Arian creed in ignorance or fear, and Hilary made the return to orthodoxy easy for them by instruction and gentleness. At the national council of Paris (361) he had practically all the bishops present, and he secured the deposition of Saturninus. In 362 he went to Italy and worked for two years there with St. Eusebius of Vercelli for the recognition of Nicaea. He presided over the Synod of Milan (364) where the orthodoxy of Auxentius the Homoean (i.e. against Homousios of Nicea) bishop of Milan was discussed, but Valentinian was imposed on by Auxentius and ordered Hilary to leave Italy. As a protest he composed *Contra Auxentium*. He returned to Poitiers and died there after six

128

years on 13 January (366 or 368). He received the title of Doctor of the Church in 1851.

St. Hilary has won the unanimous admiration of posterity and has been acclaimed by it as the *Athanasius of the West*. His strength of character, soundness of doctrine and his leadership recall Athanasius, to whom indeed he was in many ways inferior (the more troubled state of Eastern affairs gave Athanasius a broader stage on which to display his great talents), but whom he surpasses in his philosophical study of controverted questions and in the originality of his ideas. There is in his writings vigorous reasoning and deep personal conviction and a certain impetuosity which led Jerome to call him 'the Rhone of Latin eloquence'. St. Jerome classes him among the masters of eloquence.

Writings. (A) Dealing with the Arian controversies. (1) *De Trinitate*, (12 books) 356-359, in Asia Minor, to define and establish scientifically against Arianism the ecclesiastical teaching on the God-man. In Book I he tells of his conversion and explains his purpose is to combat Sabellianism and Arianism. Books 2 and 3 establish the concept of the three Persons and their real distinction from one another, and unity of nature. Books 4-12 develop the *homo-ousios, (consubstantial)* doctrine of the Second Person. 'In the domain of early ecclesiastical literature it is certainly the most imposing of all the works written against Arianism'. (2) *De Synodis*, (359), sometimes regarded as Book 13 of preceding, has two parts (a) chapters 9-65 *historical*, the different formulas of faith in various Eastern synods, and (b) dogmatic (66-91), proving to the Homoiousians that their fear of *homoousios* is groundless and that their homoiousios, *like* in nature, implies *same* in nature, implies *homoousios*. Its purpose is to secure co-operation amongst defenders of Nicene creed. (3) The *Apologetica*, replies to attacks on the mildness of *De Synodis*. (4) (a) *Liber ad Constantium Augustum* (360), in which he asks the emperor (after Seleucia) for an audience at Constantinople, to convince him of the deceit of Saturninus; when this was not granted, he wrote (b) a lively apologia to his fellow-countrymen (bishops) under the title *Contra Constantium imperatorem* (360) (Constantius favoured the Arian bishops). He compares the emperor to Nero, Decius, Maximian, denounces him as Antichrist. (c) *Contra Auxentium*. (5) A great historical work possibly entitled *Opus historicum adversus Valentium et Ursacium*. To Part I of this belongs the so-called Book I *ad Constan-*

tium which is probably a letter from the Synod of Sardica (343) to the emperor. In Part III are letters of Pope Liberius from exile.

(B) **Exegetical.** (1) Commentary on St. Matthew (355). He is a pioneer in scholarly exegesis in the West. (2) Commentary on the Psalms (364). Origen's influence is evident. (3) Treatise on Job. The Book of Mysteries (approx. 360) – part recently discovered. His correspondence has been lost. St. Jerome attributed a *Book of Hymns* to him. Three hymns have been found, celebrating the redemption of the race by the God-man. Hymns and the Book of Mysteries (part) were discovered by J. F. Gamurrini in a manuscript of Arezzo in 1887.

Doctrine. See Caryé, pp. 360-364 and Bardenhewer, p. 408, 409. The leading thought in his writings is the defence and illustration of the faith of Christians in the divinity of Jesus Christ. Father Le Bachelet says of him that he is outstanding 'for having undertaken the reconciliation of two currents which until that time had been divergent (the Latin of Tertullian, Novatian and St. Cyprian and the richer, more speculative Greek current which depended chiefly on Origen). Thus he gained a double advantage for Western theology; he enriched it with new fertile elements and at the same time helped to determine and render more precise the theological terminology of the future. But he suffered the usual fate of all pioneers; those who followed him and benefited by his labours soon surpassed him, either by their genius, such as Augustine, or by their style and clarity, such as Ambrose and Leo; his glory was outshone by theirs' (*apud* Cayré). Yet St. Hilary has been accorded his own special glory by posterity as the great champion of the Trinity, an intrepid prelate, an eloquent and zealous and kindly bishop. St. Jerome writing in 384 sums up the judgment of his contemporaries: 'The merit of his confession (of the faith), the activity of his life, and the splendour of his eloquence will be celebrated wherever the name of Rome is heard.'

HOSIUS OF CORDOVA. LUCIFER OF CALARIS

Hosius of Cordova was born about 256 and died 357, was bishop of Cordova and one of the most famous and most persecuted champions of the faith in the Western Church in its struggle against Arianism. He probably presided at Nicea (325)

130

and Sardica (343) and was possibly responsible for the term *homoousios*. He may rightly be called the 'Athanasius of the West'. Athanasius in his *Historia Arianorum*, made known a letter (355) of Hosius to Constantius who tried to detach him from his allegiance to Athanasius.

Lucifer of Calaris, bishop of Cagliari in Sardinia, for refusal to condemn St. Athanasius at the Synod of Milan (355) was banished by Constantius to the East, and remained in exile until Julian's reign (361-363). In exile and on his return he was involved in many conflicts with former friends and allies, and did the East a great disservice in consecrating Paulinus bishop of Antioch; this increased the bitterness of the Meletian schism. The terms of the Synod of Alexandria (365) were mild to penitent Arians and found no favour with him. In exile he composed several works, addressed to the emperor, including two books on St. Athanasius. 'The chief characteristic of Lucifer is his very discourteous language towards the emperor'. His style and diction are plain, he is an excellent example of contemporary Latin folkspeech and by reason of his copious scripture quotations an important witness to the pre-Jerome Bible-text.

AUSONIUS. ST. DAMASUS

Ausonius (310-395), nominally a Christian, has his place rather in the general history of Roman literature as a *poet*.

St. Damasus (366-384) was one of the most celebrated of the fourth century Popes, and cultivated the epigram with great success. At his direction St. Jerome undertook the task of making a Latin version of the Scriptures. We have many metrical epitaphs, and inscriptions for churches, poems on martyrs, and one on the conversion and martyrdom of St. Paul, also some letters.

SCHISMS AND HERESIES

Novatianism survived as a rigorist faction in the East and West. **St. Pacian,** bishop of Barcelona, assailed the fourth century adherents of it in Spain. *Donatism* – see later. *Priscillianism*, an obscure heresy, afflicted the Spanish Church from 380. It seems to have combined Gnostic dualism, Manichaeism, mythology and astrology.

ST. AMBROSE

St. Ambrose of Milan (c. 339-397), Doctor of the Church, was born of noble Christian parents at Trier, and his father, who was Praetorian Prefect for all Gaul, dying at Trier, Ambrose and the two elder children were brought to Rome by their mother. The youngest was destined for a political career and his talents marked him out for rapid advancement. In 374 he was governor of Northern Italy, residing in Milan and still a catechumen. Auxentius, Arian bishop of Milan through the favour of Valentinian I, was able to hold his position as bishop, but violent scenes between Catholics and Arians marked the attempt to elect his successor. In order to calm the agitation Ambrose entered the Church and was immediately hailed by both sides and elected bishop. Resistance proved of no avail and Ambrose was baptized at his own request by an orthodox Catholic priest on 30 November 374, and consecrated on 7 December 374. He immediately set about perfecting his theological education, and under Simplicianus, who succeeded him, devoted himself to the Christians and especially the Greek early writings – Clement of Alexandria, Origen, Basil, Didymus the Blind. He had the distinction of being instrumental in the conversion of St. Augustine and of baptizing him (387).

St. Ambrose, resembling St. Cyprian in many ways, on his election sold his property to be distributed amongst the poor, and became a model of the Christian pastor – unselfish, zealous, charitable, and like Cyprian, but on a broader stage than he, a majestic figure, a peerless orator, a firm, prudent, capable administrator, styled 'emperor among bishops'. He was accessible to all men (Augustine *Confessions* 6:3), gladsome with the glad, sorrowful with the sorrowful. Augustine has written of his oratory: 'Verbis eius suspendebar intentus... et delectabar suavitate sermonis', and he declares that it was to him chiefly his conversion under God, was due. (*Conf.* 5:13; *Ep.* 147-23). Ambrose was a friend and monitor of emperors, one of the great world-figures of his era, and the acts of his episcopate are an essential part of the history of his time. The young Gratian (375-383) loved him as a father, and to him Ambrose dedicated two treatises: *On Faith* and *On the Holy Ghost* (381), the aim of which was the eradication of Arianism. In his struggle against the Arians he turned against them a weapon of their own – religious hymns, embodying the true

132

doctrine, to be sung during the ceremonies.

His *political influence* was very great. Gratian abandoned Trier in favour of Milan, probably to have Ambrose's help, and his conduct, weak and vacillating until then, became firm and resolute. He suppressed the revenues and the immunity granted to the colleges of pagan priests, and removed the statue of the goddess Victory from the Curia. Gratian was assassinated in Gaul in 385, and the throne was seized by Maximus to the prejudice of Valentinian II, a child, whom Gratian had given a share in the empire. Justina, his mother, hastened from Sirmium to beg Ambrose's help and Ambrose went to Trier to help her cause. Meanwhile the pagans in Rome tried to obtain from the new emperor the re-establishment of the Altar of Victory, Symmachus the Prefect being their spokesman. Ambrose returned just in time to prevent the emperor from giving the verdict to Symmachus. Justina was at heart an Arian, and she brought a band of Gothic Arians to Milan and demanded for them the Portian Basilica. Ambrose refused, but a month later, Easter 385, there was an attempt to take the New Basilica by force – it failed. A fresh attempt was made in 386 and a rival to Ambrose was announced. Ambrose gathered his followers into the Portian Basilica for a siege and employed their leisure time in singing hymns. It was here he preached his famous discourse *Contra Auxentium* ('The emperor is intra ecclesiam not supra ecclesiam', – '*In* the Church not *above* the church'). The emperor finally abandoned his plan.

Maximus invaded Italy (387) and was defeated by Theodosius of Aquileia (388) and Valentinian was restored. Ambrose's relations with Theodosius were as friendly as those of Valentinian's after Justina's death in 388. Valentinian was murdered (392) by Arbogast at Vienne in Gaul. Theodosius the Great (379-395) and Ambrose clashed on two occasions, but friendly relations continued and Ambrose did not suffer any loss for his courage. Ambrose maintained the absolute independence of the Church and accorded to the emperor only the privilege of defending her. In 388 at Callinicum (Syria) Christians destroyed a synagogue and severe measures against them by Theodosius were withdrawn at Ambrose's very strong request. (He threatened Theodosius from the pulpit that Mass would not begin until he lifted the punishment.) In 390 at the instance of Ambrose the emperor did public penance for the massacre of Thessalonica (several thousands killed). Ambrose personified in this circumstance not only the Catholic Church but the conscience of humanity (Theodoret). When Valentinian was killed in 392, Ambrose was on his way to baptize him and he preached at his funeral. In his sermon he used the words so often quoted in support of baptism of desire '*si martyres suo abluuntur sanquine et hunc sua pietas abluit et voluntas*', *(If martyrs are cleansed by their blood, then Valentinian has been cleansed by his devotion and determination to follow Christ)*. He preached Theodosius's funeral oration also. Two years later he died, 397. 'On the historical background of those troubled times his person gradually emerges with all its manly charm. Although he himself went to the Greeks for his learning both his character and his conduct were for ever stamped with the mark of Rome. His iron will, his pertinacity in carrying out his plans, his sense of discipline, his practical turn of mind were all gifts of his Roman nature, and in Ambrose they reached the highest degree of force and brilliance'. (P. de Labriolle, *apud* Cayré.) He is the great champion of the rights of the Church, convinced that society could have no better mainstay than them, and was the first striking example of 'the great part that the Christian episcopacy was to play in a world which had been shattered and renewed, and for which, though he did not foresee it, he helped to pave the way'. (Duc de Broglie, *apud* Cayré). 'Ecclesiae fidelis doctor et catholicae veritatis adversum hereticos usque ad periculum sanguinis defensor acerrimus', (Faithful leader of the Church and ardent defender of the Catholic faith against heretics even at peril of life itself) (Augustine).

Works. They are chiefly exegetical, moral, and to a smaller degree dogmatic. **Exegetical.** (1) *Hexaemeron* (6 books) 387. It began as Lenten homilies and draws largely on St. Basil's works, and on Origen and Hippolytus. (2) *Genesis* – first chapters are treated in *De Paradiso* (375), *De Cain et Abel*, *De Noe et arca*, *De Abraham* (2), *De Isaac et anima*, *De Jacob et vita beata* (2), *De Joseph patriarcha*, *De Patriarchis*. (3) *De Helia et ieiunio*, *De Nabuthe Iezrelita*, *De Tobia* etc. (4) *Psalms* – twelve Sermons on (12) Psalms, and twenty-two Sermons on Psalm 118. On *Isaias* (lost). (5) *Commentary on St. Luke's Gospel* – (10 books) his longest work (389).

Moral and Ascetic. (1) *De officiis Ministrorum* (3 books) – it is modelled on Cicero's *De officiis* and discusses *honestum et utile, (the Lawful and the Good)*, as sources of obligation. (2) *Praise of virginity.* (a) *De Virginibus* (3 books) to his sister Marcellina (377). Book 3 contains a sermon given by Pope

134

Liberius, 353 (from whom in 355 Marcellina received the veil).
(b) *De Virginitate* (378). (c) *De Institutione Virginis et sanctae Mariae virginitate perpetua* (392). (d) *Exhortatio Virginitatis*, preached at Florence at the dedication of a church built by Juliana.

Dogmatic. (a) *De fide*, (5 books) to Gratian on Christ's, divinity and against the Arians (377-80). (b) *De Spiritu Sancto* – to the same (5 books, 381) on the Holy Ghost, and modelled closely on the Works of Didymus the Blind, Basil, Athanasius. (c) *De incarnationis dominicae sacramento* (381). *Expositio fidei* has been lost, and *Explanatio symboli* is of doutbful origin. (d) *De mysteriis* – a mystagogical catechesis similar to the work of St. Cyril of Jerusalem, its model. Its authenticity is no longer doubtful but *De Sacramento* is now regarded as an imitation of and subsequent to this work. (e) *De paenitentia* (2 books), 384, is a refutation of Novatianism and is of great importance for the study of the doctrine and practice of Penance in the fourth century. (See Athanasian Creed, *supra*.)

Sermons. His discourses are models of rhetorical composition (two especially, on Valentinian and Theodosius) and of capital importance for contemporary history. Only a few are extant (a) *De excessu fratris sui Satyri* (375, 378?) – a worthy memorial of a loved brother and intimate companion, a funeral oration, and a discourse *(De fide resurrectionis)* on the eighth day; (b) *De obitu Valentiniani consolatio*, (392); (c) *De obitu Theodosii oratio* (395); (d) *Sermo contra Auxentium de basilicis tradendis* (386). Valentinian at the instigation of Justina commanded that the basilicas of Milan be handed over to the Arians and their bishop (above).

Letters – 91 extant, important for history of the time, and for style. (Ep. 22 is not authentic).

Hymns. St. Ambrose was inspired by the Arians to compose hymns for the people to chant at religious services. He introduced and enriched this practice according to the manner of his Oriental contemporaries, and the custom spread from Milan to the Western Church. Four Ambrosian hymns are genuine and vouched for by St. Augustine (*Aeterne rerum conditor*, Sunday Lauds, Winter; *Deus creator omnium*; *Jam surgit hora tertia*; *Veni redemptor gentium*. These are in iambic dimeters, in strophes of four verses each, and metre and laws of quantity are rigorously observed, the diction being elevated, simple, grave, lucid. Ambrose introduced antiphonal singing – two choirs singing alternately (as was the custom in Antioch

135

and Syria). From the seventh century all hymns in the liturgy were termed Ambrosian so it is difficult to know the genuine ones. It is possible that twelve hymns in all should be attributed to him. The hymns became very popular with the faithful, unlike the more learned and complicated compositions of St. Hilary. The *Te Deum* was supposed to have been composed by St. Ambrose and St. Augustine at the latter's baptism, but it is later than these Fathers, probably fifth century and the composition of Nicetas of Remesiana. (See Altaner, s.v.)

Ambrosian Liturgy. Apart from the hymns other liturgical innovations are associated with St. Ambrose. The *Ambrosian (Milanese) rite* is indebted to him to some extent. There is a tendency to recognise the Oriental character of this (and the Gallican or Spanish Mozarabic) rite and to assign them to the middle of the fourth century. It is thought that Gaul and Spain felt the Oriental influence by way of Milan, and Duchesne tends to the belief that it was Auxentius (Arian) who led the way. P. Lejay says that Ambrose on succeeding Auxentius probably retained many of his non-doctrinal innovations. Whether he simply retained or corrected or initiated, it was Ambrose who gave his name to the rite.

Ambrosiaster (c. 366-384). *Commentaries* on thirteen epistles of St. Paul (*Hebrews* excepted) – outstanding in quality, were ascribed by all to St. Ambrose until Erasmus discovered the error. The author is now styled Pseudo-Ambrose, the work is certainly of Ambrose's time. Authors mentioned include Hilary (G. Morin), or Isaac Judaeus (Morin), or Evagrius of Antioch, or Aemilius Dexterus, St. Augustine, Pelagius. The author possibly composed *Quaestiones Veteris et Novi Testamenti*, also. The Commentary on St. Paul is an exceptionally fine work of exegesis.

PRUDENTIUS. ST. PAULINUS. SEDULIUS

Prudentius (348-405) – Aurelius Prudentius Clemens is easily the foremost among the Latin poets of Christian antiquity. He was born in Saragossa in Spain of an illustrious Christian family, entered public life and was twice president of his native province, but about the age of fifty (grey hair, 'nix capitis') gave up the splendours of the imperial court for solitude. He visited Rome after 400, and died some years later in Spain. In 405 he published a collection (7 books) of his writings that has come down to us. An eminent poet, he has been compared to Horace and, Claudian excepted, he excels his pagan contemporaries as an artist in verse. Spain produced the greatest Christian poet of this period. Prudentius at one bound surpassed all the Christian poets who preceded him. He is incontestably the greatest poet of the fourth century. What is expecially to be noticed in his work is the triumph of Christian inspiration in art. (1) *Cathemerinon Liber*, - 12 daily hymns for different periods and actions of the day. (2) Book 6 also is lyrical in character – *Peristephanon Liber* – 14 canticles in praise of the martyrs of Rome and Spain. On these two books his fame rests. Three other metrical works: *Apotheosis*, *Hamartigenia, Libri duo contra Symmachum* (possibly his most perfect work). *Psychomachia* and *Dittochaeon,* are the remaining works.

St. Paulinus of Nola was born in 353 in Bordeaux of a wealthy senatorial family, and became a disciple of the rhetorician *Ausonius* to whom he remained closely bound in friendship all his life. Through his influence he attained political eminence, but abandoned it and devoted himself to literary pursuits. His master besought him, not to become a Christian, remonstrated with him, reproached him, but he yielded to grace, sold his property and received baptism (c. 390). In 393 he was ordained priest, and in 394 retired to Nola, birthplace of his protector, St. Felix. He came to Nola with his wife, Teresa, and led there a life of prayer, mortification and poverty. He was elected bishop of Nola in 409, and exercised this office with devoted zeal and Christian generosity and self-sacrifice until his death in 431. Lacking the fire and strength, and creative force and splendid diction of Prudentius, he is gentler and milder, calm and simple, always the cultivated refined man of letters. The *correspondence* of Ausonius and Paulinus, especially that relating to the conversion, is of great charm and interest.

Carmina Natalitia, – thirteen – are compositions in hexameters in honour of St. Felix each year for thirteen years. In three paraphrases of psalms he created a new form of Christian poetry – first in iambic trimeters, second and third in hexameters. *Epithalamium Juliani et Jae*, a Christian nuptial poem. About fifty *Letters* survive.

Sedulius. Caelius Sedulius was a priest before 450. He composed a famous hexameter poem called *Paschale Carmen* (Migne PG 19, 533-754) dealing with the wonderful works of

137

Our Lord. In the dedication to one Macedonius he explains the title in conjunction with 1 Cor. 5-7. It is in five books – first dealing with the Old Testament, others with the New Testament (St. Matthew especially), the miraculous element in them. His work was highly prized in the Middle Ages for its pronounced ecclesiastical tone, its peculiar exegesis, and the simplicity and vigour of its diction'. He composed also *Paschale Opus* and two hymns, portions of which (of the second) have been adopted into the liturgy – the Christmas hymn *A solis ortus cardine* and *Crudelis Herodes Deum*.

SULPICIUS SEVERUS. TYRANNIUS RUFINUS

Sulpicius Severus (c. 420), born of a noble family of Aquitania about 363, was a friend of Paulinus and one of the most polished and refined prose-writers of his time. He abandoned the lawcourts and wealth for poverty, after his wife's death, at the entreaty of St. Martin of Tours. (1) *Chronicorum libri duo* – summary history of the Old Testament, and a compendium of ecclesiastical history of interest for its description of the Priscillianist controversies. He shows great literary ability and historical acumen. (2) *Life of St. Martin* (c. 400) – the miracles chiefly. (3) *Dialogi* – two – complete the account of the Life. Letters.

Tyrannius Rufinus, born about 345 near Aquileia, was educated there and there met St. Jerome. He travelled to Egypt in 371 and lived with the hermits of the Nitrian desert, went to Alexandria, and was a disciple of Didymus who inspired in him a great love of the Greek Fathers, Origen especially. John of Jerusalem ordained him in 390. He mentioned Jerome in an edition of Origen and Jerome denied adherence to Origen and a bitter feud ensued. Rufinus satisfied Pope Anastasius on his own orthodoxy. He left for Aquileia (398), thence to Messina where he died, 410. He is best known as a *translator from Greek* of Origen, of Pamphilus of Caesarea, of *Sententiae* of Sextus, Eusebius's *Church History*, Basil's monastic rule, works of Gregory of Nazianzus, Josephus's *Jewish War* (?) but he did more than translate, e.g. in case of Eusebius; he re-edited and translated freely. **Original Works**: *Apologia in Hieronymum* (400) two books (to which Jerome replied), *Apologia ad Anastasium* (400). *Commentary on Apostles' Creed, On the Patriarchs' Blessings*. His *Historia Ecclesiastica* (Eusebius's work in his hands became a new work) (402-403) was the first Western attempt at a history of the Church.

ST. JEROME

St. Jerome, Doctor of the Church. Sophronius Eusebius Hieronymus 349?-420, was born at Stridon, a town on the borders of Pannonia and Dalmatia. The chronology of his life is somewhat difficult but at twelve (or twenty?) years of age (367?) he went to Rome to finish his literary studies, and was an enthusiastic pupil of Aelius Donatus, cultivating the Greek and Latin classics with a passionate interest. He was attracted to the study of rhetoric and the influence is to be noted in all his works. He read avidly the Greek philosophers, and became a savant in the best sense of the word, devoting much care to the building up of a library. A naturally deep piety withdrew him from the immorality of the city after a brief acquaintance with it, and he was baptized by Pope Liberius about 365, at an early age for the time. From Rome he went to Trier, one of the best universities of the West, and was attracted to the study of theology, and resolved to become a monk. He moved on to Aquileia where he is soon to be found amongst a circle of youthful and learned friends and he remained here for six or seven years (368-374?). *Rufinus* was one of his friends. He suddenly departed from the East (374), visiting Thrace, Bithynia, Pontus, Galatia, Cappadocia and Cilicia. At Antioch he met Evagrius, future successor of Paulinus. From there he went to the East, to the desert of Chalcis, the 'Syrian Thebaid', and practised fearful austerities. He studied Greek and learned Hebrew 'not without difficulty', under the guidance of a baptized Jew. 'I alone know... what labour this study cost me, how often I lost courage, how often I abandoned and again took up my purpose' (*Ep.* 125.12). After two years he returned to Antioch and was ordained priest by Paulinus.

Constantinople. Attracted by the reputation of Gregory of Nazianzus he journeyed to Constantinople (379) to hear his sermons and he was instructed by him in the science of biblical exegesis (he had followed Apollinaris in the same subject). During the Council of Constantinople he met St. Gregory of Nyssa also. It was at this period he made his first attempt at translation and exegesis, and became well acquainted with the works of Origen. In 382 he went to Rome with Paulinus of

139

Antioch and St. Epiphanius, to a council held to end the Meletian schism in Antioch.

Rome (382-385). This short visit shaped Jerome's future life. He became secretary to Pope Damasus and wrote letters to East and West and replied to queries from all parts. At this time in Italy and especially in Rome there were complaints about the innumerable differences in the current Latin biblical texts. Damasus commissioned Jerome to establish an official text of the early Latin version then in use in the West, to put an end to the variety in texts current. This great work, begun in 384, took up his lifetime practically, gave him a definite object and an opportunity for employing to the Church's benefit the vast treasures of knowledge he had amassed. He had position and influence now and was freely spoken of as next Pope. But public opinion soon veered around, and under the lash of Jerome's tongue and pen, the Romans turned on the ecclesiastical savant of unequalled learning and the ascetic apostle of self-renouncement and self-consecration to God, for he criticised the moral life of Rome, and especially of its clergy, pitilessly. Criticism and insinuation increased daily and enemies began to speak evilly of his relations with a circle of noble Roman ladies, his disciples in the way of asceticism. The study circle met in the house of Marcella on the Aventine, and other famous names were Paula and Eustochium. When Siricius became Pope the influence of Jerome waned and he left Rome to live in Palestine, 'from Babylon to Jerusalem'.

Bethlehem (386-420). He left Rome in August 385, and Paula and her daughter, Eustochium, followed and founded a monastery of religious women. First the three visited the Holy Places, his brother Paulinianus joining them. They visited also Egypt and Alexandria and the monastic settlement of Nitria. He met Didymus the Blind. In 386 they settled at Bethlehem, and St. Paula built two monasteries, one for men under Jerome, and one for women over which she and later Eustochium presided. Jerome began to collect a library and to study Hebrew more diligently and Aramaic, taught Paula and her daughter, and taught the monks theology, and Latin classics especially Virgil. Sulpicius Severus writes: 'He is ever immersed in his studies and his books; neither night nor day does he take any rest'.

Here he was to spend the remaining thirty-five years of his life, a life extraordinarily fruitful in labours for the Church. He completed the revision of texts he had begun in Rome, but about 390, began the translation of the Bible that has made him immortal. It was finished in 405, and after two centuries was accorded first place in the West. It was given the name **Vulgate** in the thirteenth century. He brought out commentaries from 391-406, and 407-420. He gave homilies to the monks, translated Origen's homilies, engaged in historical, dogmatic and controversial work, original and translated. His correspondence for these years is most voluminous, his letters deal frequently with difficult problems and some of them on theology and exegesis and ascetics are valuable treatises in themselves. Well could Sulpicius write of him: 'he is incessantly occupied in reading or writing' (*Dial* 1-1:9).

The peace of his seclusion was broken by the wretched controversies on Origen (398-404). Jerome had been an admirer of Origen but he sided with Epiphanius against John of Jerusalem and his old friend Rufinus. '*Laudavi interpretem non dogmatisten, ingenium non fidem, philosophum non apostolum; si mihi creditis Origenistes nunquam fui; si non creditis nunc esse cessavi*', *I revered him as an exegete, not as a theologian – for his genius not his faith, as a philosopher rather than an apostle; believe me I have never been an Origenist – if you do not believe this, at least from this moment, I have ceased to be one:* (Ep. 46). Jerome was more concerned with his reputation for orthodoxy than with the question of Origen's orthodoxy. The correspondence between Jerome and Rufinus was very vigorous and disedifying and St. Augustine (*Ep.* 73) endeavoured to reconcile them. Jerome overwhelmed his adversary with biting invective of which he was absolute master. As a rule he employed this sharp weapon for better causes, e.g. the refutation of the Luciferian schismatics (378), or the attack on *Helvidius* in 383. This lay disciple of Auxentius of Milan wrote that Mary had other children beside Jesus. In 393 Jerome championed continence against the monk Jovinian, and in 404 denounced the Gallic priest *Vigilantius*, a remote forerunner of Protestantism.

St. Augustine's relations with him began unhappily. He wrote to Jerome in 394 suggesting concentration on the translations of Oriental exegetes and criticising Jerome's interpretation of the Peter and Paul Antioch incident. This letter and another did not reach Jerome but others knew of it and Jerome resented the criticisms which reached him secondhand. A friendly exchange of letters followed. A new exchange was occasioned by the *Pelagian controversy*. This controversy aroused all Jerome's wrath and satire and the defenders replied with violence to Jerome. Early in 416 a number, including monks and ecclesiastics, broke into his monastery and set fire to it. His declining years were filled with tribulations. One of his eloquent letters deals with the impression made by the news of the fall of Rome (410). (*Epp.* 126, 127). (See Father Duff's *The Letters of St. Jerome*, page 78) Eustochium died in 418 and her death was a great grief to Jerome. Worn out by vigils and fasts and warfare of the mind he died in September 419 and his body was laid near the tomb of Paula at the entrance to the Grotto of the Nativity. 'To the church he has left the precious fruits of his long-life labours in the field of Sacred Scripture and to posterity the inspiring example of the assiduous pursuit of and unswerving loyalty to the highest ideals of Christian perfection'. (Duff. o.c.).

Works. (A) on the Text of the Scriptures. *His translation of the Scriptures* is the most important and meritorious of all his works and the ripe fruit of his most painstaking studies. (a) In 383 he received the commission from Pope Damasus to establish a worthy text of the Bible, to restore the *Vetus Itala*, the old Latin, pre-Vulgate text of the Bible. Jerome revised the text of the four Gospels, and then that of the other books of the New Testament. He added a revision of the Psalter based on the Septuagint (done '*cursim, magna ex parte*', *for the greatest part in haste*). This revised text, by order of Pope Damasus, was used in the Roman liturgy. In other churches Jerome's revised Psalter was known as *Psalterium Romanum*, and until Pius V (1566-1572) it was used in all the Roman churches. It is still the text used at St. Peter's for the canonical hours and fragments of it are still found in the Missal and Breviary. The New Testament in Jerome's revision was received and has remained in the Latin Church.

(b) In Bethlehem Jerome found the original of the *Hexapla* and he revised the Old Testament according to it. He began with the Psalms and amended the *Itala* text. This Psalter text was first used in Gaul – hence called *Psalterium Gallicanum, The Gallican Psalter*. Later it was accepted in the West and is incorporated into the Roman breviary and is part of the *Vulgate*. He revised most of the Old Testament in this way but the books were lost and only Job has survived.

(c) Jerome decided to translate the Old Testament from the original Hebrew or Aramaic, and translated, in 390, Kings 1-4 Job, Prophets, Psalms. In 393 he translated the three Solomonic books, in 394 Esdras and Nehemias, Paralipomenon and Genesis, and by 405, the remaining four of the Pentateuch, Josue, Judges, Ruth, Esther, Tobias, Judith. He did not translate the deutero-canonical books, nor did he translate anew the New Testament.

The *Vulgate* thus contains the following four components:
(1) The New Testament or at least the Gospels, Jerome's first revision-work. (2) The Psalter, his second revision. (3) The Old Testament which he translated, minus the Psalter. (4) Four deutero-canonical books of which the text is that of the early Latin version.

St. Jerome aimed at reproducing the original text faithfully and accurately but not slavishly, at maintaining the traditional language of the *Vetus Itala* and the canons of good literary taste. His best are the historical books, his least meritorious *Judith* and *Tobias*, executed in a night and day respectively. Yet the version of the Solomonic books, done in three days, is excellent. Admitting errors and inexact renderings one still must say that not one of the ancient Latin versions can compare with Jerome's. It took many years before his versions superseded the current ones – the seventh century – and since the twelfth his versions inherited from the older translations the title of *Vulgate*. The text of the *Psalterium Gallicanum* was so popular and deeply rooted that Jerome's own translation could not supplant it.

(B) **Scriptural Studies.** (a) *Homilies* (73 extant) to monks at Bethlehem. (b) *Quaestiones Hebraicae in Genesim* – on philology, etc.; *Liber de nominibus Hebraicis; Liber de situ et nominibus locorum Hebraicorum* – a 'geographical lexicon'.

(C) **Commentaries** are either detached or in series. Several *detached* commentaries are extant. (a) Commentary on Ecclesiastes. (b) Commentaries on the four Epistles of St. Paul (387-389). (c) Commentary on St. Matthew. (d) Commentary on the Apocalypse. The great *series* of commentaries is devoted to the *Prophets*. They were begun with the translation from Hebrew and carried on to the end of his life – *Commentaries on the Minor Prophets* followed quickly – Daniel, Isaias (probably the *greatest of his exegetical works* 408-410 in extent and excellence), Jeremias. As an exegete Jerome is an Alexandrian. Like Origen he seeks a spiritual sense but he seeks to base it on a scientifically determined literal sense. Some of these works were done in great haste – St. Matthew e.g. in fourteen days.

(D) **Historical.** St. Jerome was known in his own day as a historian. (a) *Vita Pauli Monachi* (St. Paul of Thebes) 376, *Vita Malchi, Captivi monachi; Vita beati Hilarionis*. (b) Translation of the second part of Eusebius's *Chronicle* with addition of a third part (history from 326-379). (c) *De Viris Illustribus* (392). It may be inexact, in error frequently, incomplete, but is the first history of Christian literature. It gives valuable information on 135 writers.

(E) **Translations.** (a) Seventy-eight of Origen's Homilies. (b) Four books of Origen's *De Principiis*. (c) Paschal letters of Theophilus of Alexandria and one of St. Epiphanius. (d) Didymus's treatise *De Spiritu Sancto*, etc.

(F) **Controversial.** (a) Against John of Jerusalem. (b) Apology against Rufinus. (c) *Adversus Helvidium*. (d) *Contra Jovinianum*. (e) *Contra Vigilantium*. (f) *Dialogus adversus Pelagianos*.

(G) **His Letters** have from medieval times been regarded as the most charming of his writings. In contents and style they are attractive and elegant compositions. There are about 150 extant, 117 of them authentic, 57 are really treatises. Amongst the ascetic letters, the most celebrated, the following are noted: No. 14 to Heliodorus begging him to come to Chalcis; 22 to Eustochium exhorting her to perfection; 52 to Nepotian for whom he outlines a plan of the priestly life. The letters besides giving a splendid indication of the saint's spirituality give a clear picture of the Church of the fourth and fifth centuries. (See *The Letters of St. Jerome : A Selection*. Edited, with Introduction, by James Duff, Dublin, 1942.)

Scholar, witness to the faith, writer. St. Jerome is a Doctor of the Church and 'in so far as this title stands for a recognition of rare erudition, there is scarcely one among the Fathers to whom it is given with more justice' (Bardenhewer). We have testimonies from Orosius, John Cassian, Sulpicius Severus, St. Augustine to his immense learning. Sulpicius says there is no other writer so well-versed in Greek, Latin and Hebrew learning, that he has no rival in any branch of knowledge, and St. Augustine that he had read all or nearly all previous theological writers of the East and West. He was pre-eminent in biblical sciences and today he is recognised as 'a capable exegete, or rather a skilful philologist, a trained critic, and a translator of genius – the one man prepared for and called to a task so important and so difficult as a translation of the Scripture'. He was besides a pillar of the faith. The theological contents of Jerome's polemics are inferior to St. Augustine's anti-Pelagian writings, and in general St. Augustine is St.

Jerome's superior in depth, solidity and independence of thought, and in his influence on theological development. St. Jerome was not an original thinker like Augustine or St. Thomas Aquinas, but he defended and expounded tradition with vast erudition and unshakeable devotion and he defended especially the doctrinal authority of the Church and the magisterium, teaching authority of St. Peter's successor (Epp. 15, 16). With the exception of Lactantius no early Christian writer so stressed formal elegance and no writer except Tertullian has so strongly impressed his own very original personality on his writings. And though florid language, hyperbole, declamation mar his prose occasionally, it is truly said that 'none of the Christian Latin writers has exercised, even approximately, so marked an influence on the ecclesiastical Latinity of a later period – he has rightly been called the master of Christian prose for all later centuries' (Bardenhewer).

ST. AUGUSTINE

St. Augustine of Hippo, Doctor of the Church, 354-430. Aurelius Augustinus was born on 13 November 354 at Tagaste, a small town of Numidia, North Africa. Patricius, his father, became a Christian shortly before his death (371), while his mother Monica, saint, was a Christian and a model of Christian virtue. In the *Confessions* (bks. 1-9) he describes his intellectual and moral development from childhood to the death of his mother (387). There we read of the extraordinary talents of the boy Augustine to whom the problems that baffled his companions and teachers presented no difficulty. His father made great sacrifices to keep him at school, first at Madaura, and afterwards at the university of Carthage. In Carthage he was soon led into the luxury of the immoral life of that city but his reminiscences on this matter need not be taken too literally, for Augustine was certainly no worse than his follow-students of respectable families and probably much better than most of them. He formed an illicit union with a concubine of whom his son Adeodatus was born (372). At the age of nineteen he was deeply influenced by the *Hortensius* of Cicero and was seized with a burning love for wisdom (373) – his only regret being that the name of Christ, which, vaguely, from his childhood signified for him true wisdom – was not there. He read the Scriptures but they did not satisfy him. *Manichaeism* now

145

attracted him (374) for it claimed to lead men to the study and knowledge of truth whereas Catholicism subjected reason to faith and for nine years (374-383) he remained associated with the sect, amongst the *auditores*, hearers. Monica wept continually for her son's error, and was told by a bishop that 'it cannot be that the son of such tears should perish'. (*Conf.* 3:12-21).

Conversion. In 375 he began to teach rhetoric in Tagaste and (375) moved to Carthage where his great abilities as a teacher were immediately recognised and advancement to the highest position certain. Alypius was one of his pupils and his dearest friend. He began to lose faith in the Manichaeans, and the immorality of their *electi* and finally the failure of their alleged oracle of wisdom, Faustus of Mileve (bishop), to meet or dispel Augustine's doubts or prove himself even a man of solid culture and erudition, broke the spell. Soon after this (383) Augustine went to Rome, without his mother's knowledge, and after a short while spent in teaching rhetoric there secured the chair of rhetoric in Milan through the good offices of the prefect of Rome, Symmachus. Here he heard the sermons of the great Ambrose and was gradually led to the true Church. Ambrose made a profound impression on him, and he became more and more disposed to study the Catholic faith and to rid himself of prejudices. He determined to become a catechumen, and at the same time by the reading of Neo-Platonist treatises (translated by Marius Victorinus) his mind was raised from things of the sense-world to the world of reason, from the material to the spiritual. Yet a long conflict remained to be endured. He began to perceive something of the splendour of Christianity from the pages of St. Paul, but he was to some degree the slave of flesh and earthly glory still. Monica, who had followed him to Milan, sought to persuade him to terminate his unlawful union and enter lawful wedlock, but her pleadings were unsuccessful. Pontianus related to Augustine the story of Antony the monk, and the priest Simplicianus told him the wonderful conversion of Marius Victorinus to Christ, and as Augustine was deeply moved by these two narratives, and was in a state of wavering about his own conversion, deeply troubled in mind, one day he heard a mysterious voice (August 386): *'tolle, lege, tolle, lege,'* '*take and read*' (*Conf.* 8:12-29). He took up and read the passage (Rom. 13:13-14) 'Not in revelling and drunkenness'. At once all his doubts were at an end, and calm and peace entered his soul. He

146

gave up teaching, and in autumn 386 with his mother, his son, Alypius and some friends betook himself to an estate called Cassiciacum near Milan. At the beginning of Lent 387 he returned to Milan, and was with Adeodatus and Alypius, was instructed by Ambrose during Lent. On Easter night (24-25 April) he with the other two was baptized by St. Ambrose. A few months later he set out for Africa. Monica died at Ostia (387) and as late as 400 the memory of her death still stirred him to the keenest sorrow.

Bishop of Hippo. After his mother's death Augustine returned to Rome, and having spent a year in study there went to Carthage in 388. The *Vita Sancti Augustini*, by his friend Possidius tells us the story of his life from this point, where the *Confessions* break off.

Augustine with some friends spent about three years (388-391) near Tagaste living a life of monastic character – retirement, meditation and literary activity. Adeodatus died at this period. In 391 Augustine went on business to Hippo Regius where the fame of his piety and learning had preceded him, and he was made to consent to the reception of the priesthood at the hands of the aged Bishop Valerius. In 395 to prevent his being taken to rule any other see Valerius had him consecrated his coadjutor by the Numidian primate, Megalius of Calama, and in 396 on Valerius's death Augustine became bishop of Hippo. For thirty-five years he ruled the see of Hippo, and decorated not only it but the African Church and the whole Catholic world. He continued his monastic way of life as far as possible. He was tireless in the service of his people especially the poor. Like Ambrose he broke up and sold the Church plate to succour the needy and to redeem captives. He preached almost daily. He was constantly engaged on literary works, and found it a profitable and welcome change from his administrative duties. The needs of the time left him no alternative but to use his literary talents and incredible energy in that domain to the full. To the end of his life he was engaged in battle with the Manichaeans, the Donatists, and the Pelagians successively. He continued the literary refutation of the Manichaeans that he began in Rome.

The **Donatist schism** was a grave problem for the Church in Africa from the early years of the fourth century. The Novatians sided with the Donatists who maintained that no unholy person could be a member of Christ's Church. The Donatists held, too, that the efficacy of the sacraments depended on the

147

subjective dispositions of the minister, not merely on his orthodoxy (Novatianist position) but on his personal morality. The author of this false teaching was Donatus, bishop of Casae Nigrae in Numidia in 313. No works of his remain, and their first literary champion was Donatus the Great, schismatic bishop of Carthage (c. 355). Optatus, bishop of Mileve, Numidia, 370, wrote a large work *Contra Parmenianum Donatistam* (6 books). The schism spread and Augustine opposed it by preaching, public disputations and correspondence with the heads of the schism. Yielding reluctantly to decision of his fellow bishops because of increasing violence on the part of the schismatics, he appealed to the secular arm to suppress the sect. In June 411 the famous disputation was held at Carthage in which 286 Catholics and 279 Donatist bishops took part. Augustine was the soul of the Catholic party. He rallied the orthodox and confounded the schismatics by his arguments. The emperor Honorius in 410 decided on having such a council held, and it was held on 1st, 3rd, 8th June in A.D. 411, in the presence of the tribune Marcellinus. Petitilianus and Primianus were the chief Donatist speakers, Augustine and Aurelius of Carthage the Catholic. The Catholic victory was due to Augustine, and the sect had disappeared by the end of the century.

Pelagianism. There are two chief phases in the conflict with Pelagianism, 411-418, and from its condemnation in Rome (418) to 430, and to this conflict Augustine owes his foremost place in the history of Catholic doctrine. For an analysis of Pelagianism and the struggle against it see e.g. Cayré-Howitt, pp. 630 ff.

Pelagianism was first denounced in Africa at the Council of Carthage (411) and there Augustine went to preach against it. He pursued the campaign ceaselessly until the heresy was condemned in Rome (418) by Pope Zosimus. In 417 when Pope Innocent I replied to Africa associating himself with the African condemnation of Pelagius and Coelestius, Augustine announcing the answer from Rome, said (in a sermon): 'Inde etiam rescripta venerunt. Causa finita est. Utinam aliquando finiatur error', 'And the rescripts have come from (Rome). The case is ended. I only wish the error ended too.' His contemporaries recognised him as the God-given interpreter and defender of the Church-teaching on grace. 'Hail to thee', wrote the aged Jerome, 'The world resounds with thy praise. The Catholics admire thee as the restorer of the ancient faith'.

In 426 Augustine handed over administrative duties to Heraclius, but he was given no time for the quiet he so ardently desired. Besides the combat with Julian of Elcanum and the Semipelagians he had to contend with Arianism in the last years.

The Roman empire began to fall apart, and Roman Africa suffered severely in the dissolution of the empire. The proconsul Boniface revolted and called to his aid the Vandals of Spain. They turned the fruitful granary of Italy into a desert. The Goths of the imperial army sent against Count Boniface were accompanied by Maximinus, an Arian bishop (at Hippo), and Augustine wrote against and debated publicly with him. The Vandals, too, were Arians. Boniface eventually repented but was routed and compelled to take shelter in Hippo, where he was besieged. The town held out for three months. In the third month Augustine, now seventy-six, fell sick of a violent fever, and in his illness amid the horrors of the siege he begged God to liberate the city or give his subjects fortitude to endure, 'aut certe ut me de hoc saeculo ad se accipiat', 'or otherwise to take me to himself from this world'. He died, surrounded by his friends and disciples, 28 August A.D. 430. His body was taken to Sardinia in the course of the Vandal persecution under Trasamund (496-532) and in the eighth century Luitprandius (713-44), king of the Lombards, had it removed to Pavia where his tomb is still venerated in the church of St. Peter.

Works. Only classes of St. Augustine's work can be indicated here. The Benedictine edition logically begin with *Retractations* (2 books) and *Confessions* (13 books.).

Retractations. Towards the end of his life (427) he surveyed the whole field of his literary labours since 386 critically and drew up a chronological list of them, excepting his letters and discourses ('ninety-three works in 232 books'). He often adds information on the occasion and purpose, the meaning, scope, and gives corrections. It is a most important work for a critical study of St. Augustine but is a *re-tractatio*, a treating or discussing again, not a withdrawal.

Confessions (397) (13 books) is one of his most famous works, and one of the great books of all time. The first nine books were written to prove by his own experience the truth of a principle laid down at the beginning: *'Fecisti nos ad te, et inquietum est cor nostrum donec requiescat in te'*, *'You have made us for yourself and our heart is restless till it reposes in You'*. He depicts fully his mental development, setting forth all the intricate processes of the mind and its delicacies as only he could, all the emotions of his soul, to the year of his mother's death (387). Book 10 describes him as he was when the book was being written and 11-13 are meditations on the Genesis creation-narrative. The book is a hymn of praise to God – not a confession of faults, but a confession in the sense *confitebor tibi Domine in toto corde meo*, – *I will acknowledge you O Lord with all my heart* (Psalm 10); he says of it that the books *'et de malis et de bonis meis Deum laudant iustum et bonum atque in eum excitant humanum intellectum et affectum'*. – *'Whether of my evil deed or good will praise God who is just and good and arouse the mind and will of man towards him'*. Augustine tells of the great works of God and especially the work of salvation which God had wrought in bringing himself from sin to grace. (See *St. Augustine's Autobiography. An abridged form of the Latin text of St. Augustine's 'Confessions'*. Edited, with Introduction, by James Duff. Dublin, 1946,).

De Civitate Dei, The city of God (413-426) – 22 books – is St. Augustine's greatest work. There was a renewal of the old pagan accusations against Christians and these were charged with responsibility for all the calamities of the times (cf. Tertullian and all the early Apologists), and especially for the sack of Rome by Alaric (410) and the downfall of the Roman empire. The empire had been protected by the gods, the enemies of Christianity urged, and the overthrow of polytheism had angered the deities. Augustine besides refuting such charges undertook "to establish the true relationship of Christianity to paganism; his view embraces not only the present, but also the past and the future; the whole course of human history lies open before him and from beginning to end he interprets it with power and insight. His apology for Christianity rises at once to the dignity of a magnificent philosophy, that towers 'like an Alpine peak' over all the other apologies of Christian antiquity" (Bardenhewer). 2 Parts: (1) Books 1-10 pursue an apologetico-polemical purpose. 1-5 refute the pagan opinion that polytheism was necessary for earthly happiness. 6-10 are directed against the Neo-Platonist philosophers' contention that the worship of the gods was useful for the future life. (2) Books 11-22 are speculative and metaphysical. There are two great kingdoms in and through which goes on the development of life and humanity, *regnum Dei, regnum mundi*, – *The Kingdom of God, the Kingdom of (this) world*, and the conflict that goes on between the two forms the subject of the work. God's kingdom consists of His angels and men (just), the sum total and the essence and sign of the kingdom of this world is apostasy from God. Only here these two kingdoms overlap and interpenetrate one another, because the citizens of the former move as pilgrims among the citizens of the latter. Books 11-14 describe the origin of each kingdom as it is constituted by the creation of the angels and the fall of the apostate angels. Books 15-18 treat of the development and progress of the two kingdoms, and 19-22 their definite purpose and end. 'The work is specially valuable for the historical and archaeological excursions in which it abounds and for which he drew largely on Cicero, Varro and Jerome's recension of Eusebius's *Chronicon*' (Bardenhewer). St. Augustine exercised a profound and immense influence on posterity through his work.

(A) **Philosophical.** (1) *De pulchro et apto* (380). (2) *Contra Academicos*, 3 books (386) composed at Cassiciàcum, attacks their Scepticism. (3) *De Beata Vita* (386), a dialogue proving that happiness in life consists in the perfect knowledge of God. (4) *De ordine*, 3 books (386). (5) *Soliloquia*, 2 books on immortality. (6) *De Grammatica, De Musica*, 6 books (after 387). (7) *De Quantitate animae* (388), a dialogue on the immaterial nature of the soul. (8) *De magistro*, a dialogue between Augustine and Adeodatus. Christ is the only master.

(B) **Polemical.** (1) *De divinatione daemonum* (406-11). (2) *Adversus Judaeos*. (3) *De Haeresibus* (428), 88 heresies. (4) *Anti-Manichaean*. Against the Manichaeans and their dualism Augustine defended the existence of one principle of all things – God, and showed evil to be a negation of being having its origin in man's defective will. (a) *De moribus ecc. catholicae et Manichaeorum*, 2 books (388). (b) *De libero arbitrio*, 3 books (388). (c) *De Genesi contra Manichaeos*, 2 books. (d) *De Vera Religione* (390). (e) *De utilitate credendi*. (f) *De duabus animabus contra Manichaeos* (391) etc. etc.

(5) *Anti-Donatist*. In these Augustine defended the *ex opere operato*, efficacy of the sacraments, the teaching that in virtue of the divine power in the objective act, (and not in virtue of the meritorius act of minister or recipient), the objectively valid sacramental sign produces grace; Baptism; and the nature of the Church, a society of just and unjust. (a) *Psalmus contra partem Donati* (393), a rhythmic poem, called also *abecedarius* (each strophe begins with letters in order a, b, c, ...v). It was to give the people the history and ideas of the Donatists in simple fashion, and so that it could be sung. (b)

151

Contra epistolam Parmeniani (3 books, 400). (c) *De baptismo contra Donatistas* (7 books, 400). Augustine explains St. Cyprian's mode of action. (d) *Contra litteras Petiliani* – Donatist bishop of Cirta – 3 books, 405. (e) *Contra Cresconium grammaticum*. (f) *De unico baptismo contra Pertilianum et Constantinum*. (g) *Ad Donatistas post collationem*, etc. etc.

(6) *Anti-Pelagian* works stated and proved man's fallen nature, original sin, the necessity of redemption and grace, and won for Augustine the title 'Doctor of Grace'. (a) *Ad Marcellinum*, 3 books *de peccatorum meritis et remissione* and infant baptism (412). (b) *De spiritu et litera* to the same (412). (c) *De natura et gratia, ad Timasium et Jacobum contra Pelagium*. (d) *De gratia Christi et de peccato originali contra Pelagium et Coelestium*, 2 books (418). (e) *De praedestinatione sanctorum* and eleven other titles.

(7) *Anti-Arian* writings defended the consubstantiality of the three Divine Persons. (a) *Contra Sermonem Arianorum* (418) and (b) *Contra Maximum haerecticum Arianorum episcopum*, 2 books (427-428).

(C) **Dogmatic.** (1) *Enchiridion ad Laurentium sive de fide, spe, et caritate* ('opus vere aureum') – his only systematic account of Catholic dogma, 421, and written at the request of a layman. (2) *De fide et symbolo*, (393). (3) *De symbolo ad catechumenos*. (4) *De fide rerum quae non videntur*. (5) *De fide et operibus*. (6) *De Trinitate*, 15 books (399-415) 'iuvenis inchoavi, senex edidi', I began it while young but published it as an old man. (7) *De coniugiis adulterinis, Adulterous Unions*. (8) *De cura gerenda pro mortuis*. (9) *De diversis quaestionibus* 83 – one book, etc.

Exegetical. He used the old Latin versions of the Greek Septuagint of the New Testament, and St. Jerome's version, and corrected the Old Latin as far as he could. In his exposition of the psalms and the fourth Gospel he allegorises – in the more scientific works he follows rather the literal sense. His most important exegetical work is *De Doctrina Christiana*, (397-426) – aimed at elucidating the problems of how to investigate the meaning of the Scriptures, and how to make it known to the faithful, i.e. Hermeneutics (Books 1-3) and Christian Homiletics (Book 4).

Old Testament. Four works on Genesis (17 books) (389-415), works on the Heptateuch (the five books of Moses with Josue and Judges), Job and the Psalms.

New Testament. (a) A work explaining alleged contradictions

152

in the four Gospels (2 books). (b) On the Sermon on the Mount (c) Treatises (124) on St. John's Gospel – homilies of great beauty and depth. (d) Homilies on I John. (e) Treatises on St. Paul – Romans, Galatians. Augustine was the first to set forth the idea of a multiple literal sense, that whatever truth can be found in a phrase of Scripture was intended by the Holy Spirit. This would set serious problems for a scientific exegesis, and Augustine gives it only as his own opinion, and frequently he abandoned it.

Moral and Pastoral Works. (a) *De Agone Christiano* (c. 396), popular instruction on overcoming evil. (b) *Speculum* (427), collection of moral precepts from Scripture. (c) *DeMendacio*, (395) and *Contra Mendacium*, reject liceity of lying. (d) *De continentia* (395), *De Patientia* (418). (e) *De disciplina Christiana*, *De cantico novo*. *De utilitate ieiunii*, *De Urbis excidio* (410) (f) *De bono coniugali*, *De Sancta Virginitate*. (g) *De bono viduitatis* (414). (h) *De opere monachorum*. (i) *De catechizandis rudibus*, the earliest theory of the catechetical instruction.

Sermons. Augustine is 'the foremost ecclesiastical orator of the patristic epoch... He always seeks some better expression... clearer... larger; the words just spoken always fail to convey his thoughts and emotions satisfactorily'. His earlier sermons are more rhetorical and polished, the later 'excel in compactness of expression, logical power, and unadorned simplicity'. He delivered them first and then wrote them, and the hearers are generally taken to be rather intelligent and cultivated. Because of his fame innumerable sermons have been ascribed to him. (a) Exegetical sermons. See above – homilies. (b) 363 undoubtedly genuine *sermones* in the Benedictine edition, divided into four groups: (1) On Old and New Testament 1-183; (2) *de tempore* 184-272; (3) *de sanctis* 273-340; (4) *de diversis* 341-363. Next are *sermones dubii* (364-395) and fragmenta, and *sermones supposititii* (1-317). The researches of G. Morin, O.S.B., C. Lambe O.S.B. and A. Wilmar O.S.B. in recent years made many additions to this large collection of sermons.

Letters. 270, at least, treating of questions philosophical, theological, pastoral. They cover a period of over forty years (386-429) and vary in importance. There is little of personal matters in them. The so-called *Rule of St. Augustine* is derived from ep. 211.

Poems. Besides the *Psalmus contra partem Donati* he possibly composed *Laus cerei*. The Paschal *Exultet* is not his.

Character and Greatness. It would be impossible to give an adequate account of the literary labours of St. Augustine except in an extended survey and a token list will have to, suffice here. Steidle says of him 'S. Augustinus Tertulliani fecundum igenium, Origenis amplissimam scientiam et eruditionem, S. Cypriani sensum ecclesiasticum, maiestatem S. Ambrosii, Basilii gravitatem, Aristotelem et Platonem, ingenium Romanum cum ingenio Graeco et fervore Punico in se conciliavit – merito 'maximus orbis catholici magister' vocatur. Ex S. Augustino theologia mediaevalis totam fere suam scientiam hausit', 'St. Augustine combined in himself Tertullians fertile genius, Origen's vast knowledge and learning, St. Cyprian's sense of the Church, the majesty of St. Ambrose, Basil's gravity, Aristotle and Plato, the genius of Rome and Greece with the passion of Carthage, justly called 'the greatest teacher of the Catholic World' St. Augustine was the source from which almost the entire range of theological knowledge in the Middle Ages was derived. - The following aspects of St. Augustine's character, life, teaching, works are presented in Cayré-Howitt, pp. 660-713. 1. The man and the Saint; 2. His doctrinal method: (a) authority, (b) reason, (c) the heart. 3. Augustinian Theology: (a) Notion of theology, (b) Characteristics of his theology. 4. Doctrine (a) Existence and Nature of God, Divine attributes, (b) Trinitarian doctrine, (c) Work of God – creation and providence, (d) The Man-God, Christ, His Union with God; as Mediator; Mother of God, (e) Man – his original form, original sin and its consequences. Justification. Sanctifying grace. Actual grace. The gratuity and nature of grace. Liberty of man and efficacy of grace. Mystical graces – contemplation, wisdom, intelligence. Predestination – its difficulties and Augustine's solution. 5. Moral and ascetic teaching. 6. The Church and the Sacraments. 7. The Last Things.

Cayré classifies the essential points of St. Augustine's teaching on these matters, and concludes his review: 'history can point to no churchman more perfect than Augustine, for he combined holiness and knowledge, speculation with faith, and action with contemplation in an unparalleled degree. A great man of letters, he was still more a man of tradition and authority as well as a daring theologian and original thinker. All these great qualities enabled him to study with so much fruit the mystery of the Trinity, to build up the exact framework of Christian anthropology and the theology of grace, to

154

open up and develop fresh avenues of thought on the Church and the Sacraments and to throw new light on the traditional teaching on the last things. From another point of view he was no less outstanding as a moralist, exhorting souls to the most energetic activity under the guidance of the most intense action of God'.

No Latin Father has left so many and such extensive works as St. Augustine, and only St. Chrysostom among the Greek Fathers has contributed so much to ecclesiastical literature. His style is very attractive, he has consummate skill and readiness in expressing his thoughts and especially in setting forth the thoughts and emotions of his soul. His diction is noble and choice, but occasionally he condescends to use the popular language of the time, accommodating himself to the hearers of his sermons and discourses. His writings 'mirror a highly-gifted personality, a heart overflowing with the ardour of life and the warmth of love, a mind unparalleled for logical acuteness and speculative depth. If Jerome is rightly called the most erudite of the Fathers, Augustine is certainly the greatest, the most original and versatile' (Bardenhewer).

His mind is attracted to the obscure problems of theological anthropology such as the relations of man to God, reparation and re-union, sin, grace. In this department of theology he towers above all others as an incomparable master. Still he does not develop his ideas in a complete system, but frequently writes in answer to pressing current needs, and his works need to be read in the order of their composition. He attracted and influenced his contemporaries profoundly – his letters bear eloquent testimony to this. He was constantly appealed to for the solution of problems and to each correspondent he furnished generous and lucid responses. Posterity has hailed him as did his contemporaries, and has recognised in him as 'one of those mighty spirits that appear only at great intervals of time, but are destined to influence very profoundly the destiny of humanity. He has earned from all later generations the title of a Second Paul, a Doctor Gratiae, (Doctor of Grace). No Father of the Church has, even remotely, so magisterially affected the entire later course of philosophy and theology, as Augustine did. With princely generosity he scattered along his way ideas in which later thinkers found the materials for entire systems of doctrine; his words were often the origin of dogmatic controversies that have agitated powerfully more than one generation of mankind. Ecclesiastical authority, both conciliar and

155

pontifical, has always reckoned him among the chief doctors of the Church; it has declared that particularly in matters of divine grace its nature, necessity and gratuitous character his writings are a faithful mirror of the teachings of the Church' (Bardenhewer).

Augustine, like many of the ancient Christian thinkers, was a Platonist in philosophy, but his Platonism was coloured by the Christian religion and spirit. Plato he regards as the foremost of all pre-Christian philosophers, and Aristotle as second only to Plato. He manifests his Christian Platonism especially in demonstrating the existence of God. His argument has been abandoned by Aristotelian scholastics with the exception of St. Bonaventure. For his theology, especially of grace, see Bardenhewer, pp. 498 ff. and pp. 490-498 for his philosophy. Of his relation to the Greek Fathers, Campbell writes that in an essay on the Greek Fathers Augustine merits a considerable place 'for his career conditioned the future of the remotest thought of his time. In the intellectual formation of one to whose influence in the history of the Western ideas only Plato's and Aristotle's compare, whose domination of medieval philosophy and theology suggests the exclusiveness of a monopoly and who can yet be hailed by contemporary philosophers as the first modern man – in the mental make-up of this colossus, what is the share of the Greek Fathers? If he were only their Western mouthpiece, more effective than all others because of an arresting style and an expounding instinct superlatively adapted to the West, then the Greek Fathers were the major force in medieval and modern Christianity, hidden beneath the phrases of an African rhetorician. St. Augustine was not thus eminent as an expounder, however eminent as a stylist; he was only the mouthpiece of his own endowments as enriched by the heritage of his day'. Campbell points out that in him we meet the names of Irenaeus, Origen, Basil, Nazianzenus, Chrysostom and others, Greek doctrine quoted and appropriated. In Ambrose, Origen and Basil spoke to him. Eusebius's *Chronicon* is a source of the *City of God*. In his *De Trinitate* he expresses preference for the opinions of the Greeks. Augustine bore the impress of his times, and, while he was a catechumen, the Greek Fathers were still sovereign. 'That sovereignty in the West was to fade forever before his creative originality, but only after Augustine too had been nourished in its traditions. For over two hundred years that sovereignty had prevailed despite accumulating causes for its overthrow, until

156

the genius of Augustine joined with migrations from the North to break the Greek ascendancy. A century after Augustine's death in 430, the Greek Fathers were all but forgotten in the scenes of their long hegemony. They came to the Western Middle Ages, but chiefly in the Western tradition, hidden for the most part in the works of men who had drawn from Augustine and other disciples' (Campbell).

For a comparison between St. Chrysostom and St. Augustine as orators see Bardenhewer – Shahan § 74, 11, p. 337. St. Chrysostom was cast in a different mould, and the pulpit was more his province than it was Augustine's. He was attracted not by theory or science but by practice and life. Unlike Augustine he does not deal with the theory of priestly eloquence (except in *De Sacerdotio*). Contrast the *breviloquium, (brevity in speech)* of Augustine with the *macrologia, (length in speed)* of Chrystostom who can scarcely finish in two hours as against Augustine's fifteen or thirty minutes. Augustine took a definite theme and developed it steadily, logically, brilliantly, cogently to a goal always in view; Chrysostom is often diffuse, abandons his theme to develop a passing fancy, is less wearisome, more entertaining, and many of his sermons are in themselves gems of composition. He is less fatiguing in exposition than Augustine. He believes more in the lively image, the apt illustration, than inexorable logic. He is the more brilliant impromptu speaker, and in the exordium or peroration he seizes on some topic of the day to compel attraction. Again, Augustine seldom checks his allegorising tendency, while Chrysostom of Antioch training remains a faithful disciple of the restrained and literal exegesis and with the ease of the master in exegesis and in pulpit oratory he 'unites and reconciles science and life, mind and heart. No one has ever interpreted Holy Scripture as successfully as Chrysostom with such thoroughness and prudence, sobriety and accuracy, depth and comprehensiveness,... delicacy and refinement'. Augustine is the greater philosopher and theologian in his sermons, the greater literary artist perhaps, and if he fatigues or strains, he compensates not only by the solidity and logic of his exposition but, for his more intelligent listeners at least by his splendid antitheses, his brilliant *jeux d'esprit* and his endless playing on words'. Even to this day the Golden-Mouth is reckoned the prince of Eastern orators... with whom in the West only Augustine can compare'. But the fact that Augustine can be considered a rival to Chrysostom at all throws into relief the

157

overwhelming greatness of the African – for in the many other departments of life and letters under which Augustine can be considered, he is seen to be the rival or master of the outstanding genius in each particular sphere. No one of the Fathers has so won the minds and hearts of men of all times and all nations as the gentle, lovable Bishop of Hippo. 'Beata natio ex qua Deus omnipotens Ecclesiae talem ac tantum excitavit magistrum et doctorem' (Steidle).

See article on St. Augustine by E. Portalié in *Dictionnaire Théol. Cath.*, *A guide to the Thought of St. Augustine*, E. Portalié, S.J. London 1960, *A Monument to St. Augustine*, Editor, Father M.C. D'Arcy, S.J. 1930, and especially *Augustine the Bishop* by F. Van der Meer, English transl., 1961.

Friends and Disciples of St. Augustine include: Marius Mercator (c. 400); Orosius, A Spanish priest who was in the Pelagian controversy: St. Prosper of Aquitaine, and St. Hilary both corresponded with Augustine.

GALLIC WRITERS

John Cassian of Marseilles, died c. 435. St. Honoratus of Arles, St. Eucherius of Lyons, Hilary of Arles. *Vincent of Lerins*, Famous for his *commonitoria* (memoranda) 'to aid his weak memory and remind him... of the teachings of the Fathers'.

THE WRITINGS of ST. PATRICK (fl. 432-461?)

In the seventh century, or earlier, a collection of St. Patrick's letters was made. Of this collection, known it seems as *Liber Epistolarum Sancti Patricii Episcopi*, only two letters survive intact. The longer and more famous of these is known as St. Patrick's 'Confession' (cf. conclusion 62: '*Et haec est confessio mea antequam moriar*', *(and this is my acknowledgement (confession) before death)*. This 'open letter' gives us practically all the certain information we have about Patrick's life – but it is still more revealing regarding his character and sanctity. It was never intended as a biography, but rather as a defence of his call and mission. It is in part a *confessio peccati*, *(confession of sin)* so far as it tells of his youthful waywardness; it contains a *confessio fidei*, *(confession of faith)* also; but it is primarily a *confessio laudis, (confession of praise)* (like the *Confessions* of St. Augustine) of the Lord who did such wonders through this '*peccator rusticissimus*', *(unlettered sinner)*. '*Ego eram velut lapis qui jacet in luto profundo et venit qui potens est et in sua misericordia sustulit met et... collocavit me in summo pariete*', '*I was like a stone lying deep in mud when One who is powerful came and in his mercy lifted me and placed me on top of a wall*'. (§ 12).

The other surviving letter is of an earlier date. This *Epistola ad Milites Corotici* is a seething denunciation of the barbarity of the Welsh prince who, though a Christian, had his soldiers carry off or kill some of Patrick's beloved converts: '*Manu mea scripsi atque condidi verba ista danda et tradenda, militibus mittenda Corotici non dico civibus meis neque civibus sanctorum Romanorum, sed civibus daemoniorum... Sanguilentos sanguinare de sanguine innocentium Christianorum, quos ego in numero Deo genui*', '*I with my own hand have written and laid down those words to be given and handed on and passed on to the soldiers of Coroticus... I do not say to citizens of mine nor to citizens of the holy Romans but to the citizens of hell, that they are bloody and flowing with the blood of innocent Christians, whom I begot for God, many of them* (2).'

Patrick's character, his love and zeal, humility and strength are very vividly revealed to us in these letters of his. This is done not only by the stirring events referred to or recounted, but more so perhaps by his very manner of writing – one cannot say *style*, because there is none. 'His language is highly personal and... shows us a living person... and an extremely powerful and dynamic personality'. (C. Mohrmann, *The Latin of St. Patrick* p. 2.).

ST. LEO THE GREAT

St. Leo the Great, Doctor of the Church, (440-461). Pope Leo I and Pope Gregory I are the greatest Popes of antiquity. Between 420-430 Leo was a deacon, esteemed and influential. When Sixtus III died Leo was elected Pope and consecrated 29 September 440. It was a difficult period for Church and State. The Roman empire was overrun by barbarian hordes, and the powerful bulwark of ecclesiastical unity was in danger of collapsing because of the Monophysite heresy in the East and the Byzantine see's jealousy of Old Rome. Leo was a man born to meet the needs of the time. He saw that ecclesiastical unity must be saved by the full realisation and full development of the Roman primacy and bent all his energies to this. He pursued this purpose with prudence, firm and inflexible where doctrine was concerned, dextrous as a theologian and skilful in diplomacy. His letter to Flavian of Constantinople became the guiding star of Catholics during the Eutychian controversies. He denounced the Ephesine synod 449 as a latrocinium, it is known in history as the Robber Council, sanctioned the decrees of Chalcedon (451), while rejecting canon 28 which gave Constantinople precedence over the whole East. He induced Attila (452) to spare Rome, and Genseric (455) to spare the lives of the Romans. The temporal authority and political importance of the Holy See increased greatly and the reign of Leo opened a new epoch for the papacy. He died on 10 March 461, honoured by the Church, was soon venerated as a saint, and Benedict XIV (1754) placed him among the Doctors of the Church.

Writings. (1) **Homilies** – 96 genuine, mostly festal discourses. They are brief, solemn and elevated in style, and are admired for the purity of their diction.

(2) **Letters** – 173, of which 143 bear his name. They are official, written mainly by the papal chancery and deal with canonical or disciplinary questions, defend Church doctrine on Christ against the Monophysites, deal with the Robber-Synod of Ephesus and the Council of Chalcedon, chronology of Easter, paschal dates 444-445. *Ep. Dogmatica et Flavianum* (Tome of Flavian), was received with applause by the Chalcedon Fathers as expressing the faith of the Church. He explains in it the doctrine of one person and two natures.

ST. GREGORY THE GREAT

St. Gregory the Great, Doctor of the Church. (Pope 590-604) 'Gregory I, one of the greatest successors of St. Peter, meets us at the end of the ancient life and order, or rather on the threshold of the Middle Ages'. Leo I and he affected the ecclesiastical and civil life of their time more profoundly than any of the ancient Popes. Gregory was born in Rome A.D. 540, of noble and wealthy parents, adopted a public career and became a praetor before 571. He abandoned the glory of public life, sold his inheritance and gave portion of the money to the poor and with the rest built seven monasteries, six in Sicily and one in Rome. In the last he observed the rule of St. Benedict, but Pope Benedict I called him from it and made him cardinal-deacon, and Pelagius sent him as nuncio to the emperor Tiberius in Constantinople, from which he returned to his monastery in 584. Seeing some Anglo-Saxon youths in the slave-market he longed to go to England to bring the gospel, but was compelled by the people of Rome to abandon the idea. He became Pope and was consecrated on 3 September 590. It was a time of pestilence and famine in Italy – the Lombards were burning and slaughtering everywhere. Milan was in schism (Three Chapters controversy). Gregory with quietness and firmness restored order. 'He combined more than any other an affectionate and pleasing deference towards civil authority with firmness of purpose and energy of execution; perhaps no pope ever conceived so adequate an idea of his high office or realised it with such breadth and fullness. In fourteen years as pope he bettered the conditions of a great part of mankind and uplifted the fallen ecclesiastical state. He laid the foundations of the medieval Church and of the political power of the papacy. He believed the future belonged to the Teutonic peoples'. (Bardenhewer). In 596 he sent Augustine with forty monks to England. Clausier said that Gregory and the Middle Ages were born in the same day. His health, impaired by asceticism in his early days, was always weak, and he suffered from serious illness in the last years of his life. He died in March 604.

Writings (1) **Letters** *(Registrum Epistolarum)*, 848 extant of his fourteen years as Pope – they are in fourteen books. They reveal a tireless zeal, great statesmanship, outstanding administrative ability, the vigilance of a pastor, a father's charity, love of fatherland, zeal for the things of God.

(2) *Liber Regulae Pastoralis*, *The Pastoral Rule* gives the theory of the perfect pastor of souls. Written in 591 it was sent to John of Ravenna to explain his attempted flight from the papacy. (Cf. Gregory of Nazianzus and John Chrysostom). It was translated into Greek by Anastasius II of Antioch and into Anglo-Saxon by King Alfred.

(3) *Dialogi* in 593 – lives and miracles of Italian Fathers.

(4) *Moralia in Job*, (595) – 35 books – expounds Job in the historical, allegorical and moral sense. He is brief in the historical treatment, but the practical application was done so thoroughly that it was recognised as a thesaurus of moral theology.

161

It was begun in Constantinople.

(5) **Homilies** (22) on Ezechiel (601), forty on the Gospels, two on the Canticle of Canticles.

(6) **Liturgical.** The so-called *Sacramentarium Gregorianum* was attributed to Hadrian I by Duchesne. Certainly Gregory reformed the Sacramentary of the Roman Church – he reformed the Mass by giving the Canon its present form, and the Missal generally. He revised the antiphonary. There is no reason for rejecting the tradition that ascribes to him the permanent laws and arrangement of the liturgical melodies of the Church – *Cantus Gregorianus (Gregorian Chant)*.

St. Gregory is one of the greatest of those who have occupied the Chair of St. Peter. His writings make no pretence to elegance. Gregory found no new subtle heresies to oppose, but his was the task of reviving the sinking courage of humanity, dispelling the despair from the hearts of the conquered Romans, and tempering the ignorant arrogance of the conqueror. Less the teaching office than the healing and saving ministry of the pastor was required, and for his tremendous achievements in this sphere Gregory was beloved, venerated by his contemporaries, soon ranked as a saint, then a doctor of the Church, the perfect exemplar of the Supreme Pastor – 'Pater urbis, orbis deliciae', 'Father of the city, delight of the world'.

CONCLUSION

ST. JOHN DAMASCENE

St. John of Damascus, Doctor of the Church, c. 675-749. 'Five centuries of restless curiosity had left such a deposit of literature that the bulk of the Greek Fathers threatened the fullness of their heritage to the future' (Campbell). For two centuries there had been a decline and decay, the acme of independent theological production had been reached, and excerpts and summaries had become the substitutes for originality. After two centuries the adequate summary appeared and assured to the fame of the Greek Fathers the survival of what was best in them. John Damascene is above all a gatherer of the wisdom of the past, a compiler of what he found best in knowledge, doctrinal, ascetical, exegetical and historical. He undertook to systematise the teachings and testimony of Councils and Fathers, and to mirror in his writings the tradition of the Greek Church of former times. No one arose after him to challenge his intellectual leadership and his work the *Fountain of Wisdom* won for him a classical reputation in the East. He was also a liturgical poet of note. His services to the Church include his distinguished role in the last doctrinal conflict of the East, the Iconoclastic controversy.

Born of a distinguished family in Damascus while the city was still under the Caliphs, he succeeded his father as 'Logohtete' or civil head of the Christian population. About 716 for the faith he gave up his official position and retired to a monastery of St. Sabas near Jerusalem, where he was ordained priest. The last great Greek theologian, he treated not only of dogmatic, historical and ascetico-moral questions but wrote excellent exegetical and homiletic commentaries, composed liturgical chants of permanent worth, and became the orthodox leader in the Iconoclastic controversy. He died probably in 749 and certainly before 754 when the Iconoclastic synod anathematised his memory. He was declared Doctor of the Church by Leo XIII in 1890, and his feast is kept in the Greek Church on 4th December, in the West on 27th March.

Writings, Dogmatic. His most important work is his *Fount of Wisdom* (Pege Gnoseos), written at the suggestion of a former fellow-monk, Cosmas Melodus, who had become bishop or Maiuma. Into this he condensed all his theology and portions of it are developed in separate works. It is an assembly of the wisdom of former times, summarised with such learning and accuracy that his successors did not attempt to do more than reproduce what he had done. It exercised a profound influence on later theology. It became a *Summa* for the East, and in the West theologians such as Peter Lombard, for his *Sentences*, and St. Thomas Aquinas drew freely on it. From 1150, its first appearance in Latin, it was a store-house of tradition for the Scholastics, unequal to St. Augustine's work in influence, but indispensable. It is divided into three parts. Part I 'Philosophical Chapters' aimed at giving the best in Greek philosophy, but it confined itself to Aristotle's categories and Porphyry's five universals and so came to be known as *Dialectica*. Part II, historical, is a 'History of Heresies' and, apart from the treatment of the heresies of the Saracenes and Iconoclasts, is borrowed from the *Panarion* of Epiphanius and from Theodoret. Part III 'On the Orthodox Faith' (*De Fide Orthodoxa*), the principal and most valuable section, consists of 100 chapters and, after the manner of Lombard's *Sentences*, was divided in the West into four books: Book I dealing with God and the Trinity; Book II with creation, angels, the world, man, providence; Book III with the Incarnation; Book IV with the Resurrection and Ascension, sacraments, Mariology, saints, images, canon of Scripture, eschatology. He uses the arguments from contingency and from order in creation to prove the existence and unity of God and employs St. Gregory's concept of (circuminsession' to express the relations between the Divine Persons in the Trinity.

Polemical (mainly dogmatic in character). These are numerous and varied and it will be sufficient to list the following: *The Small Book on the Orthodox Faith; An Elementary Introduction to Dogmas; On the Holy Trinity; On the Hymn of the Trisagion* (the threefold *Sanctus* is to three persons not to the Son alone); *Dialogue against the Manichaens* (long) and *Dispute of the Orthodox John with a Manichaean* (short); *Against the Heresy of the Nestorians; On Faith Against the Nestorians; against the Monophysites, On the Composite Nature, To the Jacobite Bishop of Daraea*, and *On Two Wills in Christ*.

The most original of these works is his three discourses *Against Those who reject Images* (726-730), very similar in theme but changing in treatment as the situation developed. It defends the worship of images and expounds the permanently valid principles.

164

Ascetico-Moral. '*Sacra Parallela*', so called from the parallel treatment of vices and virtues in the third part, is his second great work, a rich assembly of texts of Scripture and the Fathers on the moral and ascetic Christian life – God, the Trinity, man, human relations. Also short works: *On the Sacred Fasts; On the Eight Spirits of Iniquity; On the Virtues and Vices.*

Historical and Exegetical. *Commentaries on the Epistles of St. Paul*, compiled from the works of St. John Chrysostom, Theodoret and St. Cyril of Alexandria. (b) 13 *homilies*, 9 authentic, important among them being three on the death and Assumption of The Blessed Virgin, and those on feasts of Our Saviour.

Poems, Hymns. He composed classical and rhythmic poetry and some of his poems became part of the Greek Liturgy. Some are to be found in modern English hymn-books, e.g. 'Come, ye faithful, raise the strain' and 'The day of Resurrection! Earth, tell it abroad'. *Idiomela* (hymn with a special melody) was composed for the office of the dead.

'Two centuries after the Greek Patristic had done its work, a man arose who could transmit its riches to a rapidly estranging world. In transmitting the work of his predecessors, however imperfectly, St. John would have been a benefactor to the unhellenic West. In transmitting it so masterfully, he became a Father to all the Church in the strictest meaning of the term, the last of those who wrote in Greek to whom the term applies unchallenged' (Campbell).

BIBLIOGRAPHY

A Literary History of Early Christianity. By C. T. Cruttwell. London 1893.

Patrology. By O. Bardenhewer. Translated from the second edition by T. J. Shahan. Freiburg im Breisgau and St. Louis, Mo., 1908.

Life and Letters in Roman Africa. By E. S. Boucher. Oxford, 1913.

Handbook of the Early Christian Fathers. By E. Leigh-Bennett. London, 1920.

Mélanges de Patrologie et d'Histoire des Dogmes. By J. Tixeront. 2a edition. Paris, 1921.

Histoire de la littérature latine chrétienne. By P. Monceaux. Paris, 1924.

The Greek Fathers. By J. M. Campbell. London, New York, 1929.

Greek Literature of the Early Christian Church. By G. Bardy. English transl. by M. Reginald. London, 1929.

The Christian Latin Literature of the First Six Centuries. By G. Bardy. English transl. by M. Reginald. London, 1930.

L'Afrique Chrétienne. By G. Bardy. Paris, 1930.

A History of Later Greek Literature. By F. A. Wright. London, 1932.

Manual of Patrology and History of Theology. By F. Cayré. Translate by H. Howitt. Paris, Tournai, Rome. 1936.

Patrologia. By B. Steidle. Freiburg im Breisgau, 1937.

Patrology. By B. Altaner. Freiburg im Breisgau, 1938 (French, Italian, English translations).

Patrologia. By A. Casamassa. Rome, 1939.

Patristique et moyen age, I-II. By J. de Ghellinck. Brussels, Paris, 1946-47.

A Handbook of Patrology. By J. Tixeront. Transl. by S. A. Raemers. London, St. Louis, 1947.

Patrology. By J. Quasten. Vol. I, 1950; vol. II, 1953; vol. III, 1960. Utrecht, Brussels.

Early Christian Creeds. By J. N. S. Kelly. London, 1950.

The Oxford Dictionary of the Christian Church. Ed. F. L. Cross. London, 1957.

166

INDEX

167

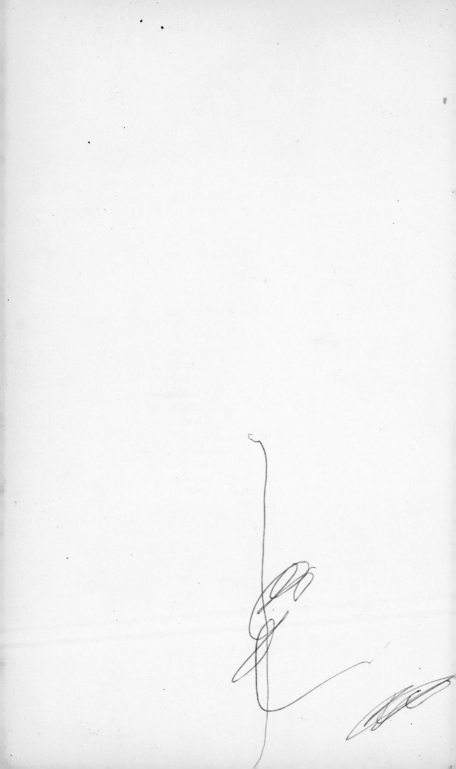